50 Off-Road Rides in the Garden State

Mountain Biking in New Jersey

D082735S

50 Off-Road Rides in the Garden State

Mountain Biking in New Jersey

Revised and Expanded Third Edition

Christopher Mac Kinnon

ISBN-10: 0-9652733-9-3
ISBN-13: 978-0-9652733-9-8

FREEWHEELING PRESS
P.O. Box 540
Lahaska PA 18931

www.freewheelingpress.com
info@freewheelingpress.com

Cover by Karen Ross **www.karenross.com**
Author cover photo by Greg Brower

Special thanks

To my father, for instilling in me an appreciation for the simplicity of the natural world.

To Cathy, for believing in this project.

And to the many county, state, and federal park employees who took the time to answer questions and review the trail routes.

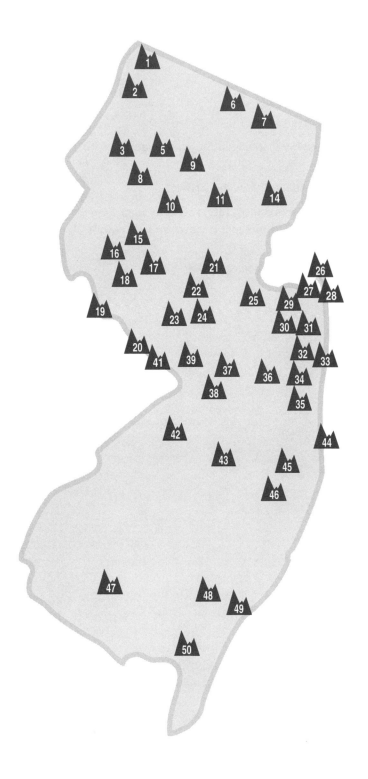

Contents

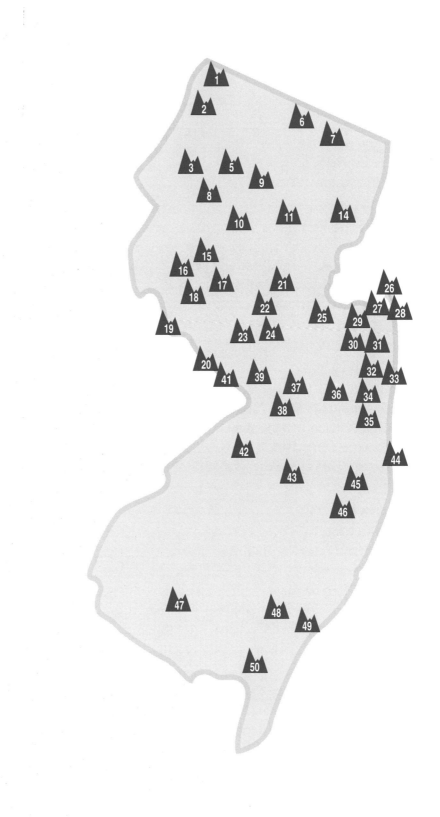

Introduction

New Jersey's sometimes under-appreciated natural beauty is nowhere as evident as on its off-road trails. The state's landscapes are many and diverse. In central New Jersey, the coastal region gradually gives way to rolling hills in the interior. Northern coastal destinations offer glimpses of New York City, while locales in the northwestern section are character-ized by mountainous terrain.

The Garden State's network of parks, recreation areas, forests, and public open spaces provides a variety of opportunities for the mountain-bike enthusiast. From nearly flat rail trails to strenuous rocky hill climbs, the rides included in this book range in difficulty from easy to expert.

New rides in this third edition of *Mountain Biking in New Jersey* include Sandy Hook and Thompson County Park in Monmouth County, Historic Smithville County Park in Burlington County, and several South Jersey destinations: the Brendan T. Byrne State Forest, Belleplain State Forest, and the Atlantic County Bikeway.

These routes range from 3 feet above sea level at Sandy Hook to 1,803 feet above at High Point, and there are rides to suit every level of interest and ability. The casual rider will enjoy both the Paulinskill Rail Trail and the Delaware and Raritan Canal. These historic trails, once used for transpor-tation, now serve as multi-use recreational trails for bikers, hikers, and equestrians.

Trails through Allaire State Park and Huber Woods County Park, char-acterized by uneven terrain, singletrack, rolling hills, and occasional trail obstacles, are well suited for the intermediate rider.

Round Valley Recreation Area and Mahlon Dickerson Reservation are representative of routes for advanced riders. Steep, rocky climbs and de-scents, frequent trail obstacles, and water crossings are typical along these routes. Suspension is highly recommended.

A concerted effort was made to evaluate the degree of difficulty for each route in this book. Factors such as trail length, current trail condi-tions, terrain, etc., were considered in the evaluation process. Before de-ciding on a route, take a moment also to consider your own level of fit-ness—this, too, is relevant to ride difficulty.

And then . . .

Enjoy!

Keep it clean: A special feature of this book

One thing for sure about off-road bicycling: Dirt happens!

You can put your clothes through the washer and hose down your bike after a messy ride, but there's not much you can do to clean a book that's covered in mud and grit. This is definitely a case where prevention is the best cure.

Mountain Biking in New Jersey has been designed so you can remove the individual maps, if you wish, and take them with you on your ride. All the information you need to find the trailhead and follow the route is printed back-to-back on a single sheet for each ride.

The pages have been designed to fit into a standard clear map protector available from retailers specializing in outdoor gear or from some office-supply stores.

For information about obtaining digital files of these maps, e-mail us at **info@freewheelingpress.com** or write to:

Freewheeling Press
P.O. Box 540
Lahaska PA 18931

Christopher Mac Kinnon

About the author

Christopher Mac Kinnon, a resident of Wall Township, N.J., enjoys both road and mountain biking and has completed several century rides.

His passion for finding new places to ride has taken him all over the Garden State, and his enthusiasm for sharing his discoveries led to this book.

He put his experience as a professional illustrator and graphic artist to good use in creating the maps that detail each route.

MAP LEGEND

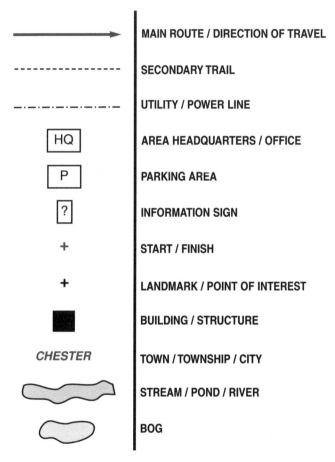

⟶	MAIN ROUTE / DIRECTION OF TRAVEL
- - - - - - - - - -	SECONDARY TRAIL
- · - · - · - · -	UTILITY / POWER LINE
HQ	AREA HEADQUARTERS / OFFICE
P	PARKING AREA
?	INFORMATION SIGN
+	START / FINISH
+	LANDMARK / POINT OF INTEREST
■	BUILDING / STRUCTURE
CHESTER	TOWN / TOWNSHIP / CITY
	STREAM / POND / RIVER
	BOG

**Because of space restrictions and for reasons of clarity,
some of the maps do not show every intersection.**

About the maps

Trail ratings

Easy

Terrain is generally flat to rolling. Routes follow wide doubletrack trails or dirt or paved trails. Occasional singletrack is possible. Trail surface ranges from cinders and packed dirt to pavement. Some areas of loose gravel and sand are possible.

Moderate

Terrain is generally rolling to hilly. Climbs and descents may be on singletrack. Trail surfaces include the above, plus small obstacles (log jumps, larger rocks, exposed roots). Expect a generally uneven trail surface.

Difficult

Terrain is generally hilly to steep and trails are primarily singletrack. Strenuous climbs and descents are likely. In addition to the small obstacles mentioned above, larger trail obstacles should be expected. Stream crossings and very rocky areas are likely. Occasional dismounts and portages may be necessary.

> Trail openings and conditions are subject to change due to weather, rerouting, reclassification, or lack of maintenance. Please keep in mind that trails are multi-use; always yield to hikers and equestrians. The routes shown on these maps are not necessarily the only way through the respective areas. Please respect both private-property and trail-closure signs where posted.

Navigation

Realizing that many cyclists either do not have cyclo-computers or find their reliability questionable, I decided to include an approximate round-trip mileage for each ride instead of providing detailed point-to-point mileage readouts. I wanted those who use these maps to feel free to explore both the designated route and nearby points of interest without worrying about exact mileage figures. The maps include directional arrows as well as natural and man-made landmarks as navigational aids. In addition, each map includes a text box describing the route and the surrounding area.

I asked several fellow riders to follow the described routes, and I have incorporated their suggestions in the final version of the maps. Their consensus was that each map is descriptive of the respective route as well as informative.

The routes indicated on these maps depict trails that were open to mountain bikes at the time they were ridden. Personal riding habits as well as possible detours and trail conditions may affect trail mileage and ratings. Meeting the needs of the many and sometimes conflicting groups of trail users may result in policy changes regarding mountain-bike usage at each area.

Please abide by current posted information. When in doubt ... ask!

–Christopher Mac Kinnon

Rules of the trail

Please ride cautiously! **No matter how carefully a bicycling route is planned, it is impossible to eliminate all potential hazards or to foresee changes in trail conditions. Bicycle riding always involves a degree of risk.**

International Mountain Bicycling Association

Rules of the trail

1. Ride on open trails only
2. Leave no trace
3. Control your bicycle
4. Always yield to non-bikers
5. Never spook animals
6. Plan ahead

and remember ...

... wear a helmet

... use courtesy and common sense

... trail riding is a privilege, not a right

... be supportive of trail-education efforts

... ride in small groups

... read posted trail signs and updates

Trail hazards:
Ticks, poison ivy, bears

Scratches and bumps may be the most common physical afflictions endured by off-road cyclists, but the farther you go from wide, paved paths, the more likely you are to encounter the health threats posed by ticks and poison ivy, both of which are common in the woods and fields of New Jersey.

The state is part of a broad area where Lyme Disease is a growing health concern. This disease, caused by bacteria, can lead to arthritis and neurological disorders, among other problems. It is transmitted by the tiny deer tick, which is the size of a poppy seed in its nymphal stage and reaches the size of a sesame seed when fully grown.

Ticks can crawl onto you when you brush against grasses, shrubs, or other vegetation, or if you sit directly on the ground or on stone walls.

The American Lyme Disease Foundation recommends taking precautions to minimize the risk of acquiring the disease.

Unfortunately, many of the recommended defenses are more easily adopted by hikers than mountain bikers. Wearing light-colored, tightly woven long pants won't appeal to many cyclists, but the foundation also advises that you

- Scan clothes and any exposed skin frequently for ticks while outdoors
- Stay on cleared, well-traveled trails
- Use insect repellant containing DEET (Diethyl-meta-toluamide) on skin or clothes if you intend to go off-trail or into overgrown areas
- Do a final, full-body tick check at the end of the day

Your chances of becoming infected with Lyme Disease are greatly reduced if you remove a tick within the first 24 hours. Early signs of Lyme Disease include flu-like symptoms and a characteristic "bull's-eye" rash, which can occur three days to a month after the tick bite. Consult your healthcare professional with any concerns you might have about Lyme Disease.

Poison ivy is a less serious health threat, but it can make you mighty uncomfortable. Some commercial products can be applied before exposure to minimize the risk of getting the rash, but the first line of defense is to simply avoid contacting the poison ivy plant. The old saying "leaves of three, let it be" is good basic advice. If you are exposed, wash yourself as soon as you can. Plain cold water will help if you are near a stream or lake. Bathing with soap and warm water is even better, but the more time passes after you are exposed, the less effective that will be.

Remember that you can get the rash not only by brushing against the plant itself, but also by touching things that have come in contact with it, including your clothes and your bike. Consider giving them a good wash, too, if you think you've been through poison ivy.

Poison ivy

If you encounter a bear

Believe it or not, New Jersey is "bear country." Black bears live here, too. Though they're concentrated in northwestern New Jersey, these large and powerful creatures have been extending their range through the northern and central part of the state to points south in recent years. The New Jersey Division of Fish and Wildlife reports bear sightings as far south as Atlantic, Cumberland, and Camp May Counties. Black bears are able to live in close proximity to humans, and their territorial preferences overlap those of mountain bikers.

What should you do if you encounter a bear?

The Division of Fish and Wildlife offers these recommendations:

- Remain calm
- Stay a safe distance away
- Leave an escape route for the bear
- Scare it away by making noise
- If the bear does not leave, move to a secure area
- Do not play dead; do not run
- Notify the proper authorities about an aggressive bear

See **www.njfishandwildlife.com** for more information about black bears in New Jersey.

Wildlife Management Areas

A patchwork of Wildlife Management Areas scattered across New Jersey provides protected habitats for fish and wildlife as well as diverse opportunities for outdoor activities including mountain biking.

The Assunpink, Black River, Capoolong, and Columbia Trail rides in this book all pass through WMAs, which are administered by the New Jersey Division of Fish and Wildlife. The division's mountain-bike policy is designed to protect these areas as well as to coordinate the activities of cyclists and hunters.

According to the rules, mountain bikes are allowed within WMAs on all roads that are open to motor vehicles on a year-round basis. Bikes may also be used on trails and secondary roads from March 1 through April 15, June 1 through September 15, and on all Sundays. (Assunpink is an exception, however; bikes are allowed there on trails and secondary roads only between June 1 and August 30, and Sunday riding is permitted during that period only.)

Mountain bikes are barred from riding on dams, cultivated fields, and lawns in any WMA. Establishing new trails is also prohibited.

High Point State Park

A stop at the 220-foot monument that crowns the highest point in New Jersey (1,803 feet above sea level) is included in this ride through High Point State Park, which offers excellent tri-state views. To the north lie the Catskill Mountains of New York; to the west, the Pocono Mountains of Pennsylvania. Much of the woodland visible to the south is part of Stokes State Forest, which can be reached via the Parker Trail (refer to the trail maps for High Point and Stokes for the connecting route).

High Point lends itself to exploration by the moderately fit as well as those looking for a strenuous outing. This ride combines sections of pavement and well-marked primitive woods roads; while not technically challenging, these roads demand a high level of physical exertion. The area is not especially well maintained, and downed trees and long rocky stretches characterize parts of these trails. For those who prefer a more leisurely ride, the park's excellent network of paved roads offers several miles of pleasurable riding opportunities.

Caution: The section of the Deckertown Turnpike (Route 650) between the Big Flatbrook and the intersection of the Appalachian Trail is quite steep. Stop by the park office for route suggestions.

Boating, fishing, and swimming are popular seasonal activities at High Point. Both the Lake Marcia and monument areas are likely to be crowded on warm-weather weekends. On the other hand, it is possible to ride long stretches of this route without encountering another rider, even when the park is relatively busy.

HIGH POINT STATE PARK

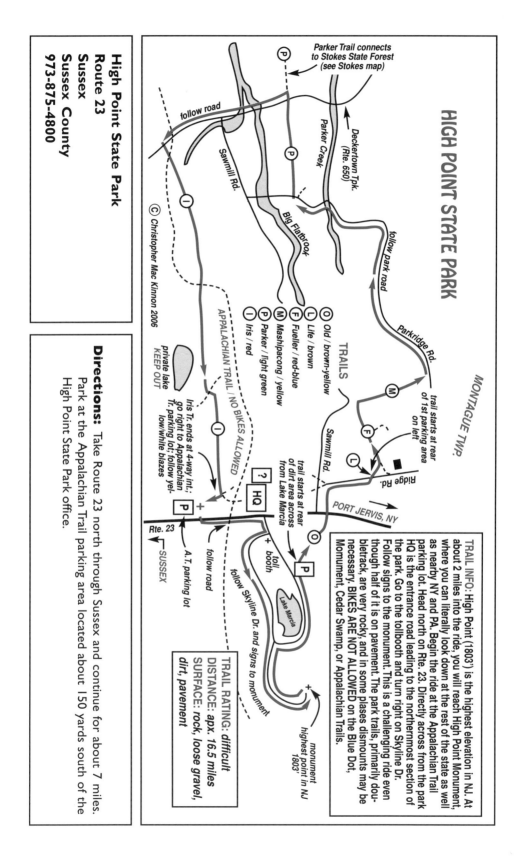

Parker Trail connects to Stokes State Forest (see Stokes map)

follow road

Deckertown Tpk. (Rte. 650)

Parker Creek

Sawmill Rd.

Big Flatbrook

follow park road

Parkridge Rd.

MONTAGUE TWP.

© Christopher Mac Kinnon 2006

APPALACHIAN TRAIL / NO BIKES ALLOWED

private lake
KEEP OUT

TRAILS

Ⓞ Old / brown-yellow
Ⓛ Life / brown
Ⓕ Fueller / red-blue
Ⓜ Mashipacong / yellow
Ⓟ Parker / light green
Ⓘ Iris / red

Iris Tr. ends at 4-way int.; go right to Appalachian Tr. parking lot; follow yellow/white blazes

trail starts at rear of dirt area across from Lake Marcia

trail starts at rear of 1st parking area on left

Sawmill Rd.

Ⓜ

Ⓕ

Ⓛ

Ridge Rd.

PORT JERVIS, NY

? **HQ** **P** +

Rte. 23

A.T. parking lot

follow road

← SUSSEX

toll booth

Ⓞ

Ⓟ

+ booth

Lake Marcia

follow Skyline Dr. and signs to monument

+ monument highest point in NJ 1803

TRAIL INFO: High Point (1803') is the highest elevation in NJ. At about 2 miles into the ride, you will reach High Point Monument, where you can literally look down at the rest of the state as well as nearby NY and PA. Begin the ride at the Appalachian Trail parking lot. Head north on Rte. 23. Directly across from the park HQ is the entrance road leading to the northernmost section of the park. Go to the tollbooth and turn right on Skyline Dr. Follow signs to the monument. This is a challenging ride even though half of it is on pavement. The park trails, primarily doubletrack, are very rocky, and in some places dismounts may be necessary. BIKES ARE NOT ALLOWED on the Blue Dot, Monument, Cedar Swamp, or Appalachian Trails.

TRAIL RATING: *difficult*
DISTANCE: *apx. 16.5 miles*
SURFACE: *rock, loose gravel, dirt, pavement*

High Point State Park
Route 23
Sussex
Sussex County
973-875-4800

Directions: Take Route 23 north through Sussex and continue for about 7 miles. Park at the Appalachian Trail parking area located about 150 yards south of the High Point State Park office.

Stokes State Forest

The present-day Stokes State Forest, with land holdings in excess of 15,000 acres, began as a 500-acre land donation by former Gov. Edward C. Stokes, who served from 1905 to 1908. Today Stokes and nearby High Point State Park, which can be reached via a connecting trail, offer a combined total of approximately 30,000 acres, most of which is accessible to mountain bikers.

The Parker Trail, which links the two areas, is shown on the High Point and Stokes trail maps. Camping is available at either park, which is convenient for hard-core riders looking for two continuous days of serious riding.

Stokes is similar to High Point in terrain and trail composition, and trails at Stokes are also lightly traveled. Most of the traffic you will encounter, whether in the form of cars, hikers, or other cyclists, will be in the vicinity of scenic Sunrise Mountain and along Kittle Road, a popular day-use area.

This entire route lies within the section of Stokes Forest that is northeast of Route 206. For information regarding trail availability southwest of Route 206, stop by the park headquarters near the trailhead.

One feature of the southern section of the park is Tillman Ravine, a natural area of small waterfalls, rock outcroppings, and hemlocks. It is off limits to bikes, but certainly worthy of exploration by foot. (Refer to park-issued map for location.)

The Tinsley Geological Trail (see map) features sections of adjoining terrain that illustrate the effects of glacial movement. You can get more information on this trail at the park headquarters.

Stokes' extensive network of trails and structures is the direct result of Civilian Conservation Corps efforts during the 1930s. They endure today as multi-use trails and facilities.

Seasonal boating, fishing, and picnicking are popular activities at Stokes State Forest.

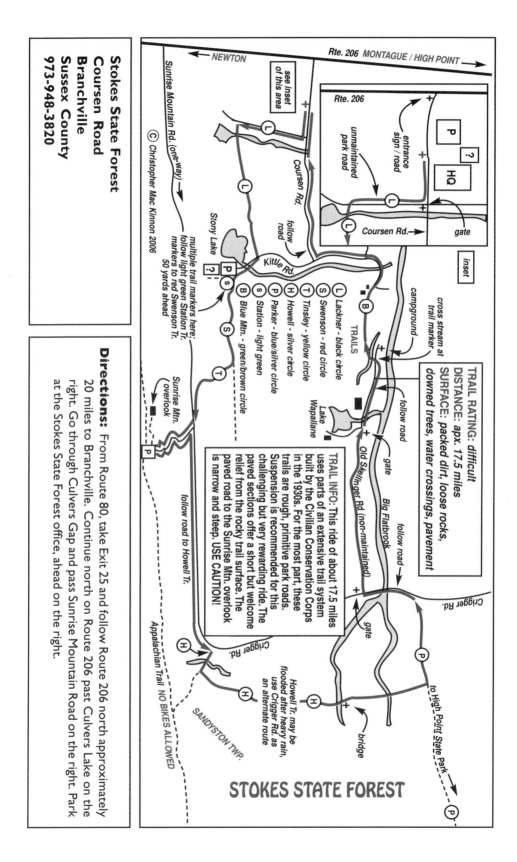

Stokes State Forest
Coursen Road
Branchville
Sussex County
973-948-3820

© Christopher Mac Kinnon 2006

Rte. 206 MONTAGUE / HIGH POINT

← NEWTON

see inset of this area

Rte. 206

entrance sign / road

P

?

HQ

unmaintained park road

L

Coursen Rd.

follow road

L

L

Coursen Rd.→

gate

inset

Sunrise Mountain Rd. (one-way)

multiple trail markers here; follow light green Station Tr. markers to red Swenson Tr. 50 yards ahead

Stony Lake

Kittle Rd.

? P S

S

S

T

cross stream at trail marker

campground

TRAIL RATING: *difficult*
DISTANCE: *apx. 17.5 miles*
SURFACE: *packed dirt, loose rocks, downed trees, water crossings, pavement*

TRAILS

Ⓛ Lackner - black circle
Ⓢ Swenson - red circle
Ⓣ Tinsley - yellow circle
Ⓗ Howell - silver circle
Ⓟ Parker - blue/silver circle
Ⓢ Station - light green
Ⓑ Blue Mtn. - green/brown circle

B

Lake Wapallane

follow road

gate

Old Skellinger Rd. (non-maintained)

Big Flatbrook

follow road

Crigger Rd.

gate

P

to High Point State Park →

P

TRAIL INFO: This ride of about 17.5 miles uses parts of an extensive trail system built by the Civilian Conservation Corps in the 1930s. For the most part, these trails are rough, primitive park roads. Suspension is recommended for this challenging but very rewarding ride. The paved sections offer a short but welcome relief from the rocky trail surface. The paved road to the Sunrise Mtn. overlook is narrow and steep. USE CAUTION!

Sunrise Mtn. overlook

P

follow road to Howell Tr.

Crigger Rd.

H

H

H

Howell Tr. may be flooded after heavy rain, use Crigger Rd. as an alternate route

H

bridge

Appalachian Trail NO BIKES ALLOWED

SANDYSTON TWP.

STOKES STATE FOREST

Directions: From Route 80, take Exit 25 and follow Route 206 north approximately 20 miles to Branchville. Continue north on Route 206 past Culvers Lake on the right. Go through Culvers Gap and pass Sunrise Mountain Road on the right. Park at the Stokes State Forest office, ahead on the right.

Paulinskill Valley Rail Trail

Scenery and serenity abound along this ribbon of rail trail that snakes its way through rural Warren and Sussex Counties. This is a New Jersey devoid of strip malls and suburban sprawl.

While the hard-core rider may opt to ride the entire described route (approximately 49 miles) in one day, we've broken the trail down into two sections, east and west, for those less ambitious. This allows the leisurely or recreational rider to complete either section without difficulty. Generally speaking, this is a lightly used trail in comparison with the Delaware and Raritan Canal, the only other off-road ride in New Jersey of comparable length.

Footbridge Park in Blairstown appears to be the unofficial "hub" for rail-trail traffic, in all likelihood because of its large parking area, its proximity to Route 94, and, of course, the park itself. Even here, trail use on weekends is moderate at worst. Unlike the Sussex Branch Rail Trail, which intersects quite a few ridable singletrack trails, the Paulinskill requires riders to remain on the trail. Most of the surrounding land is either posted or obviously private.

A side trip to Swartswood State Park via road travel is possible. There are several trails of moderate difficulty open to mountain biking at Swartswood. Inquire at the park office or call ahead (973-383-5230) for current trail conditions.

To get to Swartswood from the Paulinskill Trail: At the intersection of the Paulinskill Trail and Route 622 (on the eastern trail map), go left, follow the road over Paulinskill Lake, and continue for about 1.5 miles to Swartswood State Park. Follow signs to the park office.

The Paulinskill follows a railbed last used as a working railroad in 1963. For most of its length, its surface of cinders and dirt is conducive to all but road bikes. Expect some minor trail erosion between Cedar Ridge Road and Henfoot Road (in the western section), as well as some slightly overgrown stretches as you near the eastern terminus of the trail near Sparta Junction (in the eastern section).

Paulinskill trail sign

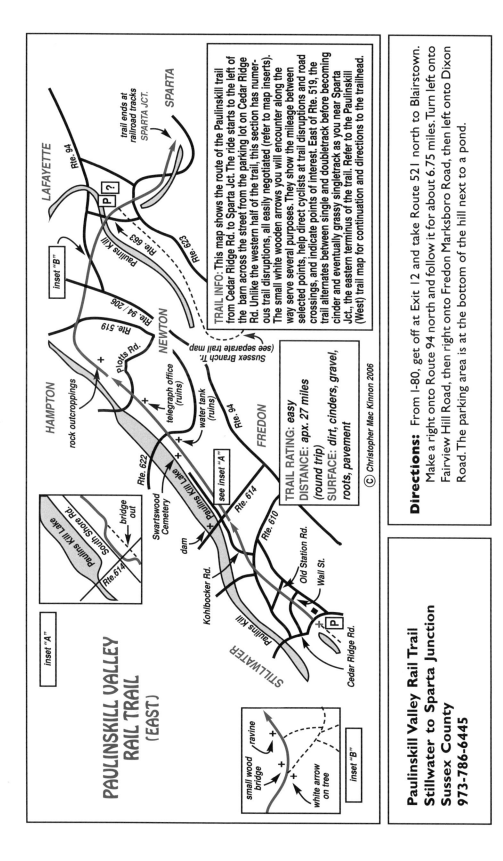

PAULINSKILL VALLEY RAIL TRAIL (EAST)

inset "A"

inset "B"

inset "A"
Paulins Kill Lake
South Shore Rd.
Rte. 614
bridge out
Rte.614

inset "B"
ravine
small wood bridge
white arrow on tree

TRAIL INFO: This map shows the route of the Paulinskill trail from Cedar Ridge Rd. to Sparta Jct. The ride starts to the left of the barn across the street from the parking lot on Cedar Ridge Rd. Unlike the western half of the trail, this section has numerous trail disruptions, all easily negotiated (refer to map inserts). The small white wooden arrows you will encounter along the way serve several purposes. They show the mileage between selected points, help direct cyclists at trail disruptions and road crossings, and indicate points of interest. East of Rte. 519, the trail alternates between single and doubletrack before becoming cinder and eventually grassy singletrack as you near Sparta Jct., the eastern terminus of the trail. Refer to the Paulinskill (West) trail map for continuation and directions to the trailhead.

© Christopher Mac Kinnon 2006

TRAIL RATING: *easy*
DISTANCE: *apx. 27 miles (round trip)*
SURFACE: *dirt, cinders, gravel, roots, pavement*

LAFAYETTE
SPARTA
Rte. 94
trail ends at railroad tracks
SPARTA JCT.
P ?
Paulins Kill
Rte. 663
Rte. 623
NEWTON
Rte. 94/206
Rte. 519
Plots Rd.
HAMPTON
rock outcroppings
Sussex Branch Tr. (see separate trail map)
telegraph office (ruins)
water tank (ruins)
Rte. 94
FREDON
Rte. 622
Paulins Kill Lake
Swartswood Cemetery
dam
Kohlbocker Rd.
see inset "A"
Rte. 614
Rte. 610
Old Station Rd.
Wall St.
STILLWATER
Paulins Kill
P
Cedar Ridge Rd.

Paulinskill Valley Rail Trail
Stillwater to Sparta Junction
Sussex County
973-786-6445

Directions: From I-80, get off at Exit 12 and take Route 521 north to Blairstown. Make a right onto Route 94 north and follow it for about 6.75 miles. Turn left onto Fairview Hill Road, then right onto Fredon Marksboro Road, then left onto Dixon Road. The parking area is at the bottom of the hill next to a pond.

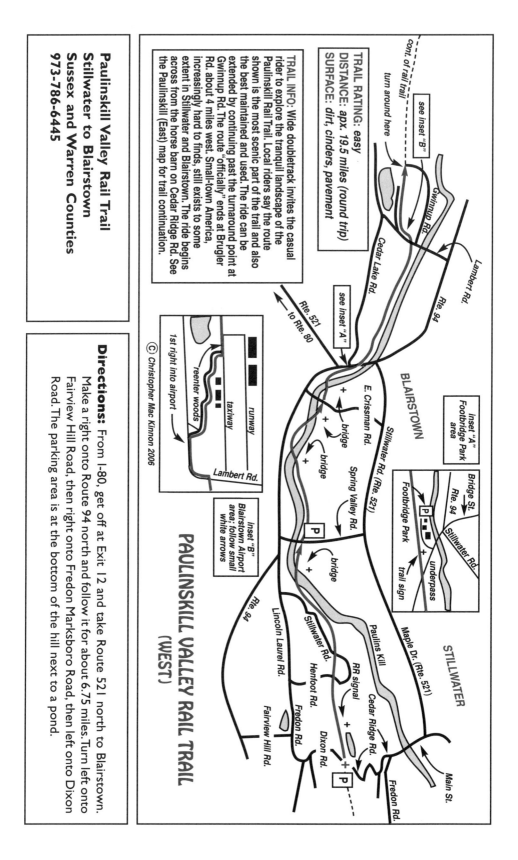

Paulinskill Valley Rail Trail
Stillwater to **Blairstown**
Sussex and Warren Counties
973-786-6445

TRAIL RATING: easy
DISTANCE: apx. 19.5 miles (round trip)
SURFACE: dirt, cinders, pavement

TRAIL INFO: Wide doubletrack invites the casual rider to explore the tranquil landscape of the Paulinskill Rail Trail. Local riders say the route shown is the most scenic part of the trail and also the best maintained and used. The ride can be extended by continuing past the turnaround point at Gwinnup Rd. The route "officially" ends at Brugler Rd. about 4 miles west. Small-town America, increasingly hard to finds, still exists to some extent in Stillwater and Blairstown. The ride begins across from the horse barn on Cedar Ridge Rd. See the Paulinskill (East) map for trail continuation.

© Christopher Mac Kinnon 2006

Directions: From I-80, get off at Exit 12 and take Route 521 north to Blairstown. Make a right onto Route 94 north and follow it for about 6.75 miles. Turn left onto Fairview Hill Road, then right onto Fredon Marksboro Road, then left onto Dixon Road. The parking area is at the bottom of the hill next to a pond.

PAULINSKILL VALLEY RAIL TRAIL
(WEST)

cont. of rail trail

turn around here

see inset "B"

Gwinnup Rd.

Lambert Rd.

Cedar Lake Rd.

Rte. 521
to Rte. 80

see inset "A"

Rte. 94

BLAIRSTOWN

inset "A"
Footbridge Park area

E. Crissman Rd.

bridge
bridge

Stillwater Rd. (Rte. 521)

Spring Valley Rd.

P

bridge

inset "B"
Blairstown Airport area; follow small white arrows

1st right into airport

reenter woods

taxiway

runway

Lambert Rd.

Bridge St.
Rte. 94

Footbridge Park

P

trail sign

underpass

Stillwater Rd.

STILLWATER

Maple Dr. (Rte. 521)

Paulins Kill

RR signal

Cedar Ridge Rd.

Stillwater Rd.

Lincoln Laurel Rd.

Henfoot Rd.

Fredon Rd.

Fairview Hill Rd.

Dixon Rd.

P

Rte. 94

Fredon Rd.

Main St.

Sussex Branch
Kittatinny Valley State Park

This ride through the rural countryside of Sussex County combines a portion of the 21-mile Sussex Branch Rail Trail with a loop through adjoining Kittatinny Valley State Park. The Sussex Branch is similar in some respects to the nearby Paulinskill Valley Rail Trail, although long segments of the Sussex Branch run through state-owned parkland or forest, while the Paulinskill borders private land for most of its length.

Toward its southern terminus, the Sussex Branch consists of several unconnected sections. In some areas the trail is well maintained and easy to follow, but unfortunately that is not the case everywhere.

Park-issued maps are posted at the Route 206 trailhead, and they can also be obtained at the Kittatinny headquarters. They describe the entire route of both the Sussex Branch and Paulinskill trails. A map of Kittatinny Valley State Park showing its network of singletrack and doubletrack trails is also available at the park headquarters.

After the trail crosses Route 206 north of Andover, where this ride begins, it continues uninterrupted to Route 616 south of Newton, the turnaround point. From here, follow the route back to a stone wall and turn there onto a dirt road leading to Kittatinny park headquarters and through the park.

The landscape of Kittatinny is a microcosm of rural Sussex County, featuring dense forests, tranquil meadows, and rugged rock outcroppings. Kittatinny State Park was once a privately owned estate with its own airport, but the state acquired this land in 1994. Its landscape is a microcosm of rural Sussex County, featuring dense forests, tranquil meadows, and rugged rock outcroppings. Lake Aeroflex is the deepest glacial lake in New Jersey.

The trailhead for this ride is on the northbound side of Route 206 about half a mile north of milepost 104. Currently without a sign, it can be recognized as a dirt area across from an abandoned barn with a circular section of concrete silo.

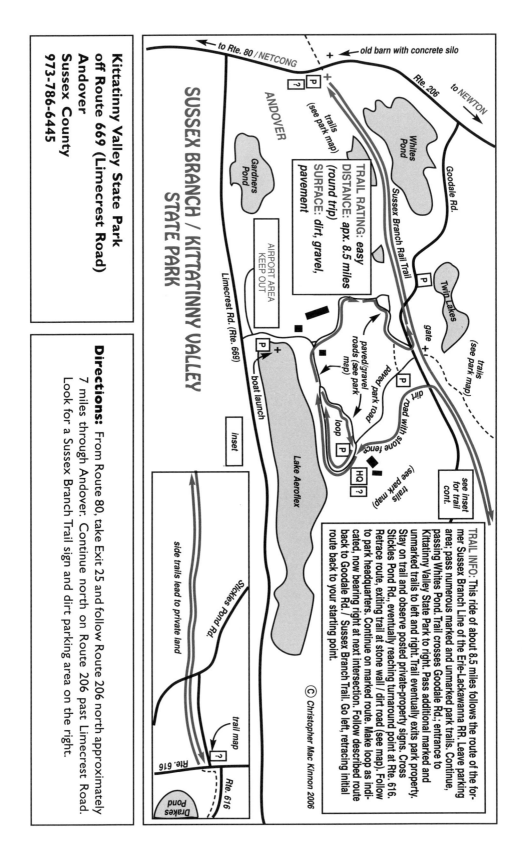

SUSSEX BRANCH / KITTATINNY VALLEY STATE PARK

TRAIL RATING: easy
DISTANCE: apx. 8.5 miles
(round trip)
SURFACE: dirt, gravel, pavement

to Rte. 80 / NETCONG

old barn with concrete silo

Rte. 206

to NEWTON

ANDOVER

Whites Pond

Goodale Rd.

Sussex Branch Rail Trail

Gardners Pond

Twin Lakes

gate

trails (see park map)

see inset for trail cont.

AIRPORT AREA KEEP OUT

paved/gravel roads (see park map)

paved

dirt road with stone fence

loop

Limecrest Rd. (Rte. 669)

boat launch

Lake Aeroflex

HQ

trails (see park map)

inset

TRAIL INFO: This ride of about 8.5 miles follows the route of the former Sussex Branch Line of the Erie-Lackawanna RR. Leave parking area; pass numerous marked and unmarked park trails. Continue, passing Whites Pond. Trail crosses Goodale Rd.; entrance to Kittatinny Valley State Park to right. Pass additional marked and unmarked trails to left and right. Trail eventually exits park property. Stay on trail and observe posted private-property signs. Cross Stickles Pond Rd., eventually reaching turnaround point at Rte. 616. Retrace route, exiting trail at stone wall / dirt road (see map). Follow to park headquarters. Continue on marked route. Make loop as indicated, now bearing right at next intersection. Follow described route back to Goodale Rd. / Sussex Branch Trail. Go left, retracing initial route back to your starting point.

© Christopher Mac Kinnon 2006

side trails lead to private land

Stickles Pond Rd.

trail map

Rte. 616

Rte. 616

Drakes Pond

Kittatinny Valley State Park
off **Route 669 (Limecrest Road)**
Andover
Sussex County
973-786-6445

Directions: From Route 80, take Exit 25 and follow Route 206 north approximately 7 miles through Andover. Continue north on Route 206 past Limecrest Road. Look for a Sussex Branch Trail sign and dirt parking area on the right.

Wawayanda State Park

Before it became a state park in 1963, Wawayanda's vast natural resources provided a source of income for the iron and logging industries. Present-day Wawayanda is a prime location for outdoor recreation in northern New Jersey.

Wawayanda, located near the New York border, has a reputation for being more "biker friendly" than many other locations. Forest roads built for use by loggers are now part of this 13,000-acre park's extensive system of trails, most of them open to mountain bikers. The variety of terrain encountered along these trails is diverse, including lush woods, rock outcroppings, and wetlands.

The focal point for many visitors to the park is 250-acre Wawayanda Lake with its scenic backdrop of forested hills. The lake is open for swimming in the summer, and there are changing facilities nearby. Canoes and boats with electric motors are also allowed, and fishing is popular. A nearby charcoal blast furnace serves as a reminder of a once-thriving iron industry (see map for location). If you simply want to cycle, park at the first lot next to the park headquarters and you'll avoid paying a toll for lake parking.

Before beginning your ride, stop in at the park headquarters for information on trail conditions, revisions, etc.

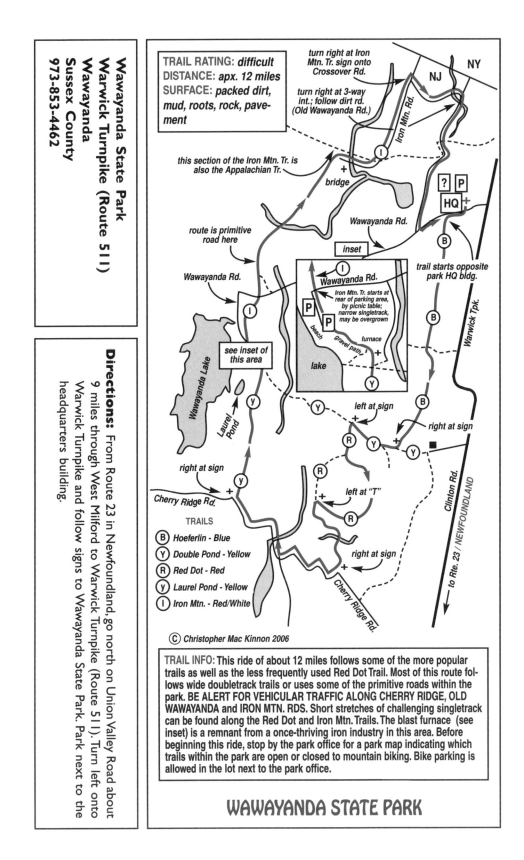

Wawayanda State Park
Warwick Turnpike (Route 511)
Wawayanda
Sussex County
973-853-4462

Directions: From Route 23 in Newfoundland, go north on Union Valley Road about 9 miles through West Milford to Warwick Turnpike. Turn left onto Warwick Turnpike and follow signs to Wawayanda State Park. Park next to the headquarters building.

TRAIL RATING: *difficult*
DISTANCE: *apx. 12 miles*
SURFACE: *packed dirt, mud, roots, rock, pavement*

turn right at Iron Mtn. Tr. sign onto Crossover Rd.

NY

NJ

turn right at 3-way int.; follow dirt rd. (Old Wawayanda Rd.)

Iron Mtn. Rd.

this section of the Iron Mtn. Tr. is also the Appalachian Tr.

bridge

? P

HQ

Wawayanda Rd.

route is primitive road here

inset

trail starts opposite park HQ bldg.

Wawayanda Rd.

Iron Mtn. Tr. starts at rear of parking area, by picnic table; narrow singletrack, may be overgrown

Wawayanda Rd.

P

P

Warwick Tpk.

beach

gravel path

furnace

see inset of this area

lake

Wawayanda Lake

Laurel Pond

left at sign

right at sign

Clinton Rd.

right at sign

left at "T"

Cherry Ridge Rd.

to Rte. 23 / NEWFOUNDLAND

right at sign

Cherry Ridge Rd.

TRAILS

- (B) *Hoeferlin - Blue*
- (Y) *Double Pond - Yellow*
- (R) *Red Dot - Red*
- (y) *Laurel Pond - Yellow*
- (I) *Iron Mtn. - Red/White*

© *Christopher Mac Kinnon 2006*

TRAIL INFO: This ride of about 12 miles follows some of the more popular trails as well as the less frequently used Red Dot Trail. Most of this route follows wide doubletrack trails or uses some of the primitive roads within the park. BE ALERT FOR VEHICULAR TRAFFIC ALONG CHERRY RIDGE, OLD WAWAYANDA and IRON MTN. RDS. Short stretches of challenging singletrack can be found along the Red Dot and Iron Mtn. Trails. The blast furnace (see inset) is a remnant from a once-thriving iron industry in this area. Before beginning this ride, stop by the park office for a park map indicating which trails within the park are open or closed to mountain biking. Bike parking is allowed in the lot next to the park office.

WAWAYANDA STATE PARK

Ringwood State Park

At 5,000 plus acres, Ringwood State Park is one of the larger tracts of public land in northeastern New Jersey. The fact that it can be described as "mountain-bike friendly" makes it even more attractive as an off-road cycling destination.

In addition to the described route, many other trails are available for riding. Among these is the rugged singletrack racecourse maintained by a local cycling club. At most marked trail intersections, trail usage and availability will be indicated. Look for brown markers with symbols indicating which activities are allowed on the respective trail. Please keep in mind that both trail usage and permitted activities are subject to change or revision.

The English country-style mansion Skylands Manor, located in the northern section of the park, is modeled after an English estate home of 400 years ago. Tours are available here and at the park's other country house, called Ringwood Manor. You can stop at the park office for detailed information about the park's facilities.

The New Jersey State Botanical Gardens occupy approximately 1,100 acres of the park. Although part of the described route passes through this area, cyclists must stay on the paved road indicated on the map. Off-road riding is strictly forbidden in this area.

Seasonal hunting, swimming, and boating are among other recreational opportunities at Ringwood.

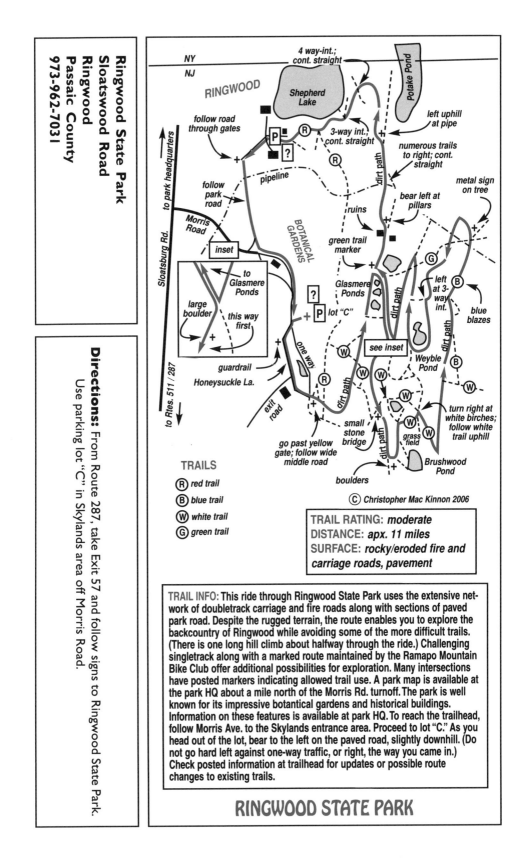

Ringwood State Park
Sloatswood Road
Ringwood
Passaic County
973-962-7031

Directions: From Route 287, take Exit 57 and follow signs to Ringwood State Park. Use parking lot "C" in Skylands area off Morris Road.

4 way-int.;
cont. straight

Potake Pond

RINGWOOD

Shepherd Lake

NY
NJ

follow road through gates

P

R

left uphill at pipe

3-way int., cont. straight

numerous trails to right; cont. straight

to park headquarters

R

?

pipeline

dirt path

follow park road

Morris Road

ruins

bear left at pillars

metal sign on tree

Sloatsburg Rd.

inset

BOTANICAL GARDENS

green trail marker

G

to Glasmere Ponds

Glasmere Ponds

left at 3-way int.

B

blue blazes

large boulder

this way first

?

P lot "C"

see inset

dirt path

B

Weyble Pond

W

guardrail

Honeysuckle La.

one way

+

R

W

W

dirt path

W

W

turn right at white birches; follow white trail uphill

to Rtes. 511 / 287

exit road

go past yellow gate; follow wide middle road

small stone bridge

dirt path

W

grass field

W

boulders

Brushwood Pond

TRAILS

(R) red trail
(B) blue trail
(W) white trail
(G) green trail

© Christopher Mac Kinnon 2006

TRAIL RATING: *moderate*
DISTANCE: *apx. 11 miles*
SURFACE: *rocky/eroded fire and carriage roads, pavement*

TRAIL INFO: This ride through Ringwood State Park uses the extensive network of doubletrack carriage and fire roads along with sections of paved park road. Despite the rugged terrain, the route enables you to explore the backcountry of Ringwood while avoiding some of the more difficult trails. (There is one long hill climb about halfway through the ride.) Challenging singletrack along with a marked route maintained by the Ramapo Mountain Bike Club offer additional possibilities for exploration. Many intersections have posted markers indicating allowed trail use. A park map is available at the park HQ about a mile north of the Morris Rd. turnoff. The park is well known for its impressive botanical gardens and historical buildings. Information on these features is available at park HQ. To reach the trailhead, follow Morris Ave. to the Skylands entrance area. Proceed to lot "C." As you head out of the lot, bear to the left on the paved road, slightly downhill. (Do not go hard left against one-way traffic, or right, the way you came in.) Check posted information at trailhead for updates or possible route changes to existing trails.

RINGWOOD STATE PARK

Mahlon Dickerson Reservation

With over 3,000 acres, the Mahlon Dickerson Reservation seems more like a state forest than a county-run facility. Deer, beaver, and black bear are among the animals that reside in this heavily wooded reservation.

Located in northwestern Morris County, it is generally regarded as the number-one mountain-bike destination within the Morris County Park System. In addition to the yellow trail, which is officially designated for bike use, the route described here uses several other trails, including the white-blazed Pine Swamp Trail and the 2.5-mile Ogden Mine Railroad bed, built to serve iron mines in the area. Highlights of the ride include picturesque Saffin Pond and the highest elevation in Morris County (1,395 feet).

Mahlon Dickerson's system of marked trails includes a section of the recently designated Highlands Trail. Please respect official trail-usage signs and, if necessary, refer to posted park maps for alternate routes.

Trail usage is generally light to moderate here, for several reasons. First, most trails at Mahlon Dickerson can be classified as difficult, the exception being the Ogden Mine Railroad bed. Also, the park is located in the less populated part of Morris County. (A small portion of the rail trail extends into neighboring Sussex County.) And finally, the size of the park means that there are more than enough trails to accommodate many riders.

In addition to the described route, many other loop rides are possible; refer to park-posted maps at Saffin Pond. Morris County trail maps are among the most reliable in accurately representing trail configurations, updates, and the locations of structures and geographical features.

Note: Trail usage and designation are currently being debated by various groups of trail users. At the time of publication, the Morris County Parks Commission was trying to develop a solution acceptable to all parties. It is likely that this process will affect several parks in the Morris County system, including Mahlon Dickerson, Patriots' Path, and Lewis Morris. Before beginning your ride, check the information sign at the Saffin Pond parking lot for the latest developments.

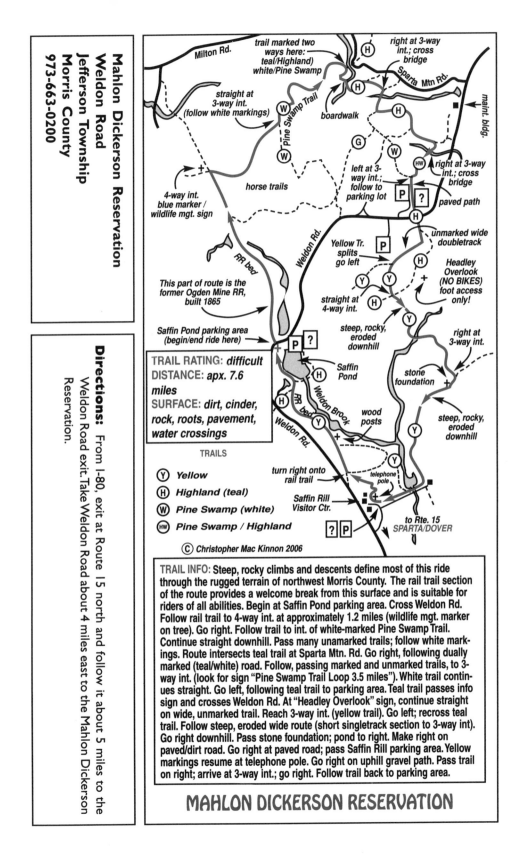

Mahlon Dickerson Reservation
Weldon Road
Jefferson Township
Morris County
973-663-0200

Directions: From I-80, exit at Route 15 north and follow it about 5 miles to the Weldon Road exit. Take Weldon Road about 4 miles east to the Mahlon Dickerson Reservation.

Milton Rd.

trail marked two ways here:
teal/Highland white/Pine Swamp

right at 3-way int.; cross bridge

Sparta Mtn Rd.

straight at 3-way int. (follow white markings)

Pine Swamp Trail

boardwalk

maint. bldg.

right at 3-way int.; cross bridge

paved path

4-way int. blue marker / wildlife mgt. sign

horse trails

left at 3-way int.; follow to parking lot

RR bed

This part of route is the former Ogden Mine RR, built 1865

Weldon Rd.

Yellow Tr. splits go left

unmarked wide doubletrack

Headley Overlook (NO BIKES) foot access only!

Saffin Pond parking area (begin/end ride here)

straight at 4-way int.

right at 3-way int.

TRAIL RATING: *difficult*
DISTANCE: *apx. 7.6 miles*
SURFACE: *dirt, cinder, rock, roots, pavement, water crossings*

Saffin Pond

steep, rocky, eroded downhill

stone foundation

steep, rocky, eroded downhill

Weldon Brook

RR bed

wood posts

Weldon Rd.

TRAILS

Ⓨ **Yellow**
Ⓗ **Highland (teal)**
Ⓦ **Pine Swamp (white)**
(HW) **Pine Swamp / Highland**

turn right onto rail trail

Saffin Rill Visitor Ctr.

telephone pole

to Rte. 15 SPARTA/DOVER

© *Christopher Mac Kinnon 2006*

TRAIL INFO: Steep, rocky climbs and descents define most of this ride through the rugged terrain of northwest Morris County. The rail trail section of the route provides a welcome break from this surface and is suitable for riders of all abilities. Begin at Saffin Pond parking area. Cross Weldon Rd. Follow rail trail to 4-way int. at approximately 1.2 miles (wildlife mgt. marker on tree). Go right. Follow trail to int. of white-marked Pine Swamp Trail. Continue straight downhill. Pass many unmarked trails; follow white markings. Route intersects teal trail at Sparta Mtn. Rd. Go right, following dually marked (teal/white) road. Follow, passing marked and unmarked trails, to 3-way int. (look for sign "Pine Swamp Trail Loop 3.5 miles"). White trail continues straight. Go left, following teal trail to parking area. Teal trail passes info sign and crosses Weldon Rd. At "Headley Overlook" sign, continue straight on wide, unmarked trail. Reach 3-way int. (yellow trail). Go left; recross teal trail. Follow steep, eroded wide route (short singletrack section to 3-way int). Go right downhill. Pass stone foundation; pond to right. Make right on paved/dirt road. Go right at paved road; pass Saffin Rill parking area. Yellow markings resume at telephone pole. Go right on uphill gravel path. Pass trail on right; arrive at 3-way int.; go right. Follow trail back to parking area.

MAHLON DICKERSON RESERVATION

Allamuchy Mountain State Park

Although neighboring Waterloo Village is the prime tourist attraction in the area and definitely worth a visit, it's the natural area at Allamuchy Mountain State Park that is of interest to the mountain biker.

Allamuchy is geologically similar to neighboring High Point State Park and Stokes State Forest, but the network of trails at Allamuchy avoids both the steepness and rocky trail surface characteristic of these parks.

The relatively isolated Deer Park Pond, which is along the described route, offers a quiet respite. Both bass and pickerel are to be found in its tranquil waters. The nearby Musconetcong River offers some of the best trout fishing in the state. Seasonal deer hunting is also allowed in the Allamuchy Natural Area; check posted information regarding seasonal openings and regulations.

Allamuchy's system of marked trails includes a section of the Highlands Trail. Please respect official trail-usage signs and, if necessary, refer to posted park maps for alternate routes.

The 19th-century Waterloo Village restoration, located on the Morris Canal and known for its summertime music performances, includes a working mill complex as well as a collection of historic buildings. Both the village (973-347-0900) and the park headquarters at adjacent Stephens State Park are located on nearby Waterloo Road (Route 604). The northern portion of Allamuchy park, which consists for the most part of rough unmarked trails, can be reached from Route 80 by exiting onto Route 206 north. Take the jughandle for International Drive and make a right at the first intersection. Follow this road for approximately 0.5 miles to a T-intersection at Waterloo Road. The heavily eroded parking area is straight across the intersection. This is also the southern terminus of the Sussex Branch Trail.

On your left as your ride along the rail trail, you'll find numerous steep and rough trails leading into Allamuchy's northern section. (Trails to the right generally lead to Jefferson Lake or the area around it.) Please respect posted private property signs in this area.

You can expect to get lost here. Unlike the Allamuchy Natural Area, this section of the park is poorly marked and relatively unmaintained.

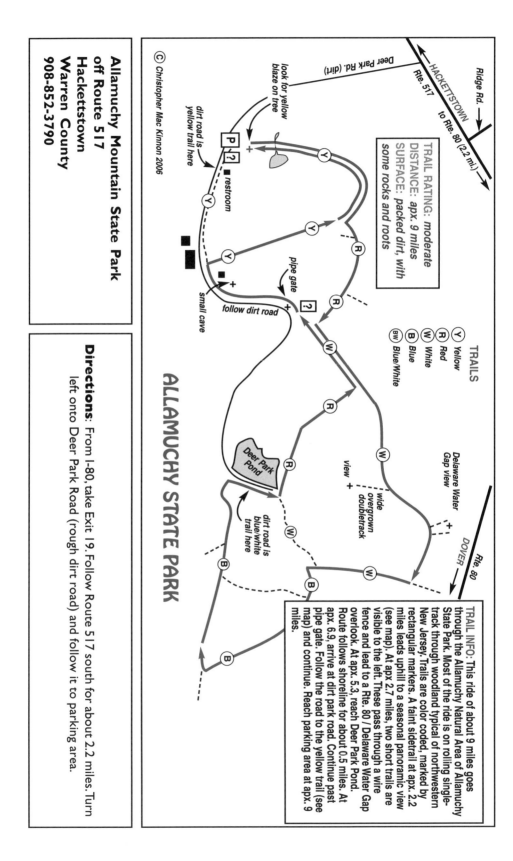

ALLAMUCHY STATE PARK

TRAILS

- (Y) Yellow
- (R) Red
- (W) White
- (B) Blue
- (BW) Blue/White

TRAIL RATING: *moderate*
DISTANCE: *apx. 9 miles*
SURFACE: *packed dirt, with some rocks and roots*

© Christopher Mac Kinnon 2006

Ridge Rd.

to Rte. 80 (2.2 mi.)

HACKETTSTOWN

Rte. 517

Deer Park Rd. (dirt)

look for yellow blaze on tree

dirt road is yellow trail here

P ?

■ restroom

Y

Y

Y

Y

R

R

R

R

W

W

W

W

?

small cave

+ follow dirt road

pipe gate

wide overgrown doubletrack

view +

Delaware Water Gap view

DOVER

Rte. 80

Deer Park Pond

dirt road is blue/white trail here

B

B

B

TRAIL INFO: This ride of about 9 miles goes through the Allamuchy Natural Area of Allamuchy State Park. Most of the ride is on rolling single-track through woodland typical of northwestern New Jersey. Trails are color coded, marked by rectangular markers. A faint sidetrail at apx. 2.2 miles leads uphill to a seasonal panoramic view (see map). At apx. 2.7 miles, two short trails are visible to the left. These pass through a wire fence and lead to a Rte. 80 / Delaware Water Gap overlook. At apx. 5.3, reach Deer Park Pond. Route follows shoreline for about 0.5 miles. At apx. 6.9, arrive at dirt park road. Continue past pipe gate. Follow the road to the yellow trail (see map) and continue. Reach parking area at apx. 9 miles.

Allamuchy Mountain State Park
off Route 517
Hackettstown
Warren County
908-852-3790

Directions: From I-80, take Exit 19. Follow Route 517 south for about 2.2 miles. Turn left onto Deer Park Road (rough dirt road) and follow it to parking area.

Black River Wildlife Management Area

State-owned fish and game lands constitute a sizable portion of the public land holdings in New Jersey. They are distinctly different in planning and purpose from state parks or state forests.

The state-issued guidebook to these areas that have been set aside for hunting and fishing describes little in the way of established trails or facilities. Navigation is at best difficult, and perhaps intentionally so.

The Black River Wildlife Management Area just north of Chester is more conducive to mountain biking than most. Here you will find two obvious paths that serve as the main arteries through the area. The first is the well-maintained rail trail that parallels the Black River, which is now part of the ever-expanding Patriot's Path. Uphill from it and running in a similar direction is a primitive utility road used to service power lines. Most of the described route makes use of these two trails.

Centrally located at Black River is a shotgun range, and you can expect to hear resounding echoes from the facility as you pedal along the route. A section of the utility road excluded from the described ride passes directly below the area; this route has been laid out to avoid it.

Although the ride is rated as intermediate overall, the rail trail is suitable for all riders. Traffic is minimal on the rail trail at Black River, even on weekends, and practically non-existent on both the utility road and connecting trails.

The nearby village of Chester, at the intersection of Routes 24 and 206, is bustling with activity on weekends. Quaint shops, boutiques, and eateries line its attractive main street.

(See page 21 for more information on the WMA system, including the New Jersey Fish and Wildlife Division's official policies on riding in these areas.)

Black River Wildlife Management Area

off Route 206

Chester

Morris County

908-879-6252

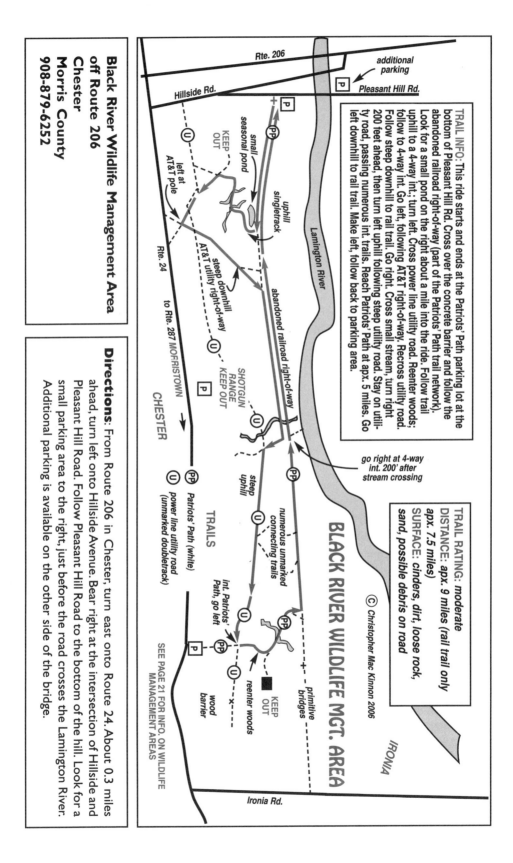

TRAIL INFO: This ride starts and ends at the Patriots' Path parking lot at the bottom of Pleasant Hill Rd. Cross over the concrete barrier and follow the abandoned railroad right-of-way (part of the Patriots' Path trail network). Look for a small pond on the right about a mile into the ride. Follow trail uphill to a 4-way int. Go left, turn left. Cross power line utility road. Reenter woods; follow to 4-way int. Go left, following AT&T right-of-way. Recross utility road. Follow steep downhill to rail trail. Go right. Cross small stream, turn right 200 feet ahead, then turn left uphill following steep utility road. Stay on utility road, passing numerous int. trails. Reach Patriots' Path at apx. 5 miles. Go left downhill to rail trail. Make left, follow back to parking area.

TRAIL RATING: *moderate*
DISTANCE: *apx. 7.5 miles (rail trail only apx. 9 miles)*
SURFACE: *cinders, dirt, loose rock, sand, possible debris on road*

© Christopher Mac Kinnon 2006

Rte. 206

additional parking

Pleasant Hill Rd.

Hillside Rd.

small seasonal pond

KEEP OUT

left at AT&T pole

Rte. 24

uphill singletrack

steep downhill

AT&T utility right-of-way

to Rte. 287 MORRISTOWN

CHESTER

SHOTGUN RANGE KEEP OUT

Lamington River

abandoned railroad right-of-way

go right at 4-way int. 200' after stream crossing

BLACK RIVER WILDLIFE MGT. AREA

IRONIA

steep uphill

numerous unmarked connecting trails

int. Patriots' Path, go left

reenter woods

KEEP OUT

primitive bridges

wood barrier

TRAILS

PP — Patriots' Path (white)

U — power line utility road (unmarked doubletrack)

SEE PAGE 21 FOR INFO. ON WILDLIFE MANAGEMENT AREAS

Ironia Rd.

Directions: From Route 206 in Chester, turn east onto Route 24. About 0.3 miles ahead, turn left onto Hillside Avenue. Bear right at the intersection of Hillside and Pleasant Hill Road. Follow Pleasant Hill Road to the bottom of the hill. Look for a small parking area to the right, just before the road crosses the Lamington River. Additional parking is available on the other side of the bridge.

Trail information sign at Lewis Morris County Park

Lewis Morris County Park

This ride at Lewis Morris County Park begins and ends at the Sunrise Lake parking lot, which serves as the focal point for a variety of park activities, including swimming, boating, and fishing, as well as mountain biking. Cyclists will find easy access here to the network of park trails including Patriots' Path (see separate maps).

Figuring out which trails are actually open to bicycles can be confusing, however. The official 1993 park map does not indicate the redesignation of several trails including the yellow "mountain-bike trail." To get the latest information on trails, cyclists should refer to updated posted information, which might include a revised map. Also, neighboring Morristown National Historic Park limits bike usage to paved roads. Look for posted signs along the Lewis Morris route around milepost 3.9 indicating the boundary line between the two parks. A portion of the Patriots' Path, which is included in the Lewis Morris route, is also closed to bikes once it crosses into Morristown National Historic Park.

Trail usage at Lewis Morris ranges from moderate to heavy, and conflicts may occur. While not as physically demanding as Mahlon Dickerson Reservation, Lewis Morris does have its share of trail obstacles and varied surfaces, loose gravel, exposed roots, and occasional wet spots. In conjunction with Patriots' Path, it can provide a full-day outing for the intermediate-level rider.

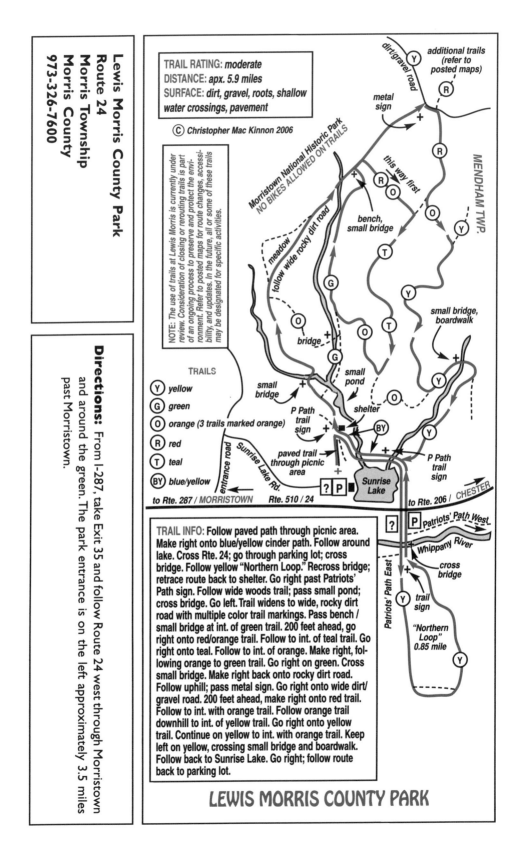

Lewis Morris County Park
Route 24
Morris Township
Morris County
973-326-7600

Directions: From I-287, take Exit 35 and follow Route 24 west through Morristown and around the green. The park entrance is on the left approximately 3.5 miles past Morristown.

TRAIL RATING: *moderate*
DISTANCE: *apx. 5.9 miles*
SURFACE: *dirt, gravel, roots, shallow water crossings, pavement*

© Christopher Mac Kinnon 2006

NOTE: The use of trails at Lewis Morris is currently under review. Consideration of closing or rerouting trails is part of an ongoing process to preserve and protect the environment. Refer to posted maps for route changes, accessibility, and updates. In the future, all or some of these trails may be designated for specific activities.

Morristown National Historic Park
NO BIKES ALLOWED ON TRAILS

MENDHAM TWP.

additional trails (refer to posted maps)

metal sign

this way first

bench, small bridge

small bridge, boardwalk

follow wide rocky dirt road

meadow

bridge

small bridge

small pond

shelter

P Path trail sign

paved trail through picnic area

P Path trail sign

CHESTER

TRAILS

Y yellow
G green
O orange (3 trails marked orange)
R red
T teal
BY blue/yellow

entrance road
Sunrise Lake Rd.

to Rte. 287 / MORRISTOWN   Rte. 510 / 24

Sunrise Lake

to Rte. 206 / CHESTER

Patriots' Path West
Whippany River

Patriots' Path East

cross bridge

trail sign

"Northern Loop" 0.85 mile

TRAIL INFO: Follow paved path through picnic area. Make right onto blue/yellow cinder path. Follow around lake. Cross Rte. 24; go through parking lot; cross bridge. Follow yellow "Northern Loop." Recross bridge; retrace route back to shelter. Go right past Patriots' Path sign. Follow wide woods trail; pass small pond; cross bridge. Go left. Trail widens to wide, rocky dirt road with multiple color trail markings. Pass bench / small bridge at int. of green trail. 200 feet ahead, go right onto red/orange trail. Follow to int. of teal trail. Go right onto teal. Follow to int. of orange. Make right, following orange to green trail. Go right on green. Cross small bridge. Make right back onto rocky dirt road. Follow uphill; pass metal sign. Go right onto wide dirt/gravel road. 200 feet ahead, make right onto red trail. Follow to int. with orange trail. Follow orange trail downhill to int. of yellow trail. Go right onto yellow trail. Continue on yellow to int. with orange trail. Keep left on yellow, crossing small bridge and boardwalk. Follow back to Sunrise Lake. Go right; follow route back to parking lot.

LEWIS MORRIS COUNTY PARK

Patriots' Path

Patriots' Path is a linear park first envisioned about 20 years ago, when Morris County officials began working to create a continuous multi-use trail connecting parklands as well as recreational and cultural facilities. Foreseeing future development in the area, these far-sighted planners also sought to preserve the land surrounding the Whippany and Raritan Rivers as a buffer between the natural environment and the new construction that would take place.

Today, Patriots' Path is a visible testament to their efforts. The routes shown on the Patriots' Path (East) and Patriots' Path (West) trail maps represent the longest currently developed and bike-accessible portions of this expanding trail. Future plans call for the path to extend as a continuous route from the Lenape Trail in Essex County to Stephens State Park in Hackettstown in Warren County. A map of the entire trail system, both existing and proposed, is available from the Morris County Park Commission, which can be reached at 973-326-7600.

Recent trail development includes the addition of the railroad right-of-way through the Black River Wildlife Management Area (see Black River trail map). For Patriots' Path trail updates, refer to current maps posted at the trailhead parking lot (see map), or stop by the Morris County Park Commission office located on Route 24 about a half mile past the entrance to the Lewis Morris County Park.

Patriots' Path could be described as "suburban" in character, especially in the western section. You'll feel in places as if you were riding in someone's backyard—or at least, as is actually the case, right next to it! Since most of Patriots' Path does border on private land, bicyclists should make an effort to stay on the trail. This is a multi-use trail best suited for leisurely riding, and cyclists can expect to encounter both pedestrian and equestrian traffic along the route and should show courtesy to other trail users.

Although classified as "easy" overall, our Patriots' Path (West) route does contain several areas that are subject to erosion damage, as well as a number of small hills that present slightly more difficult riding conditions. There is one steep hill climb about 0.25 miles into the ride along the eastern route. (See trail information box for details.)

47

Patriots' Path trail marker

Limited parking is available at the trailhead on Route 24 across from Lewis Morris County Park or in the Sunrise Lake parking lot at Lewis Morris (the starting point for the Lewis Morris route; see map for that ride). If you park at Lewis Morris, go past the "No Outlet" sign at the end of the lot. Follow the paved path slowly through the picnic area and you'll find Patriots' Path at the bottom of the hill. Follow it to the right (white blazes) and you'll reach Route 24 and the Patriots' Path parking lot approximately 0.3 miles ahead.

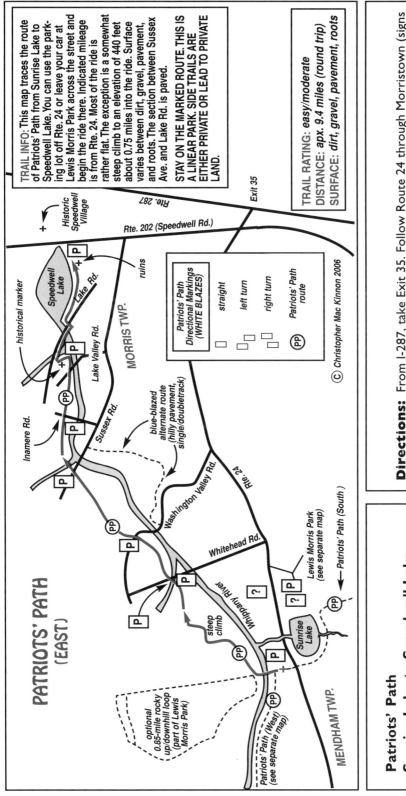

PATRIOTS' PATH
(EAST)

TRAIL INFO: This map traces the route of Patriots' Path from Sunrise Lake to Speedwell Lake. You can use the parking lot off Rte. 24 or leave your car at Lewis Morris Park across the street and begin the ride there. Indicated mileage is from Rte. 24. Most of the ride is rather flat. The exception is a somewhat steep climb to an elevation of 440 feet about 0.75 miles into the ride. Surface varies between dirt, gravel, pavement, and roots. The section between Sussex Ave. and Lake Rd. is paved.

STAY ON THE MARKED ROUTE. THIS IS A LINEAR PARK. SIDE TRAILS ARE EITHER PRIVATE OR LEAD TO PRIVATE LAND.

TRAIL RATING: *easy/moderate*
DISTANCE: *apx. 9.4 miles (round trip)*
SURFACE: *dirt, gravel, pavement, roots*

Historic Speedwell Village

Rte. 287

Exit 35

Rte. 202 (Speedwell Rd.)

historical marker

Speedwell Lake

Lake Rd.

ruins

Inamere Rd.

Lake Valley Rd.

MORRIS TWP.

Sussex Rd.

Patriots' Path Directional Markings (WHITE BLAZES)

straight
left turn
right turn
Patriots' Path route

© *Christopher Mac Kinnon 2006*

blue-blazed alternate route (hilly pavement, single/doubletrack)

Washington Valley Rd.

Rte. 24

Whitehead Rd.

Whippany River

steep climb

Lewis Morris Park (see separate map)

Patriots' Path (South)

Sunrise Lake

optional 0.85-mile rocky up/downhill loop (part of Lewis Morris Park)

Patriots' Path (West) (see separate map)

MENDHAM TWP.

Directions: From I-287, take Exit 35. Follow Route 24 through Morristown (signs may read 24/124). Look for the entrance to Lewis Morris Park on the left and the Patriots' Path parking area on the right, about 3.5 miles west of I-287.

Patriots' Path
Sunrise Lake to Speedwell Lake
Morris County
973-326-7600

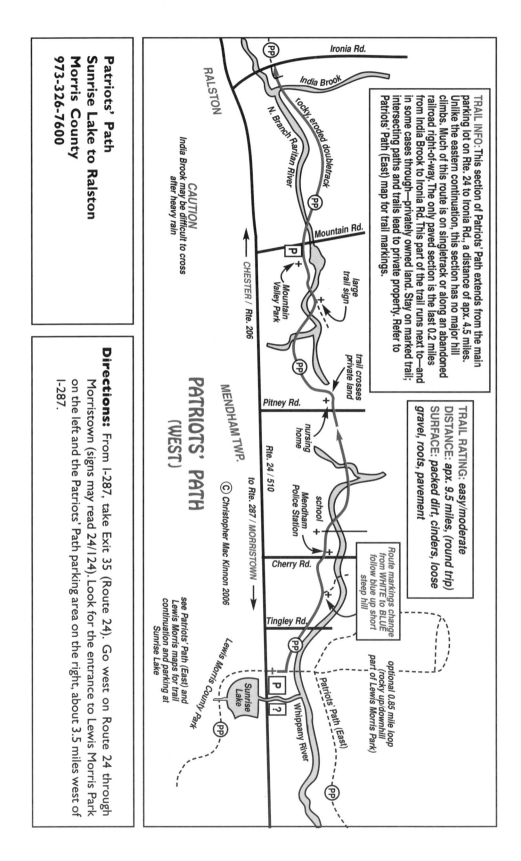

Patriots' Path
Sunrise Lake to Ralston
Morris County
973-326-7600

TRAIL INFO: This section of Patriots' Path extends from the main parking lot on Rte. 24 to Ironia Rd., a distance of apx. 4.5 miles. Unlike the eastern continuation, this section has no major hill climbs. Much of this route is on singletrack or along an abandoned railroad right-of-way. The only paved section is the last 0.2 miles from India Brook to Ironia Rd. This part of the trail runs next to—and in some cases through—privately owned land. Stay on marked trail; intersecting paths and trails lead to private property. Refer to Patriots' Path (East) map for trail markings.

TRAIL RATING: *easy/moderate*
DISTANCE: *apx. 9.5 miles, (round trip)*
SURFACE: *packed dirt, cinders, loose gravel, roots, pavement*

CAUTION
India Brook may be difficult to cross after heavy rain

Ironia Rd.

India Brook

RALSTON

rocky, eroded doubletrack

N. Branch Raritan River

PP

PP

PP

Mountain Rd.

CHESTER / Rte. 206

P +
Mountain Valley Park

large trail sign

+

trail crosses private land

PP

Pitney Rd. +

MENDHAM TWP.

© Christopher Mac Kinnon 2006

nursing home

Rte. 24 / 510

to Rte. 287 / MORRISTOWN

PATRIOTS' PATH
(WEST)

school +

Mendham Police Station

+

Cherry Rd.

Route markings change from WHITE to BLUE (only) follow blue up short steep hill

Tingley Rd.

PP

optional 0.85 mile loop (rocky up/downhill part of Lewis Morris Park)

Patriots' Path (East)

Lewis Morris County Park

see Patriots' Path (East) and Lewis Morris maps for trail continuation and parking at Sunrise Lake

+
P
?
Sunrise Lake

Whippany River

PP

PP

Directions: From I-287, take Exit 35 (Route 24). Go west on Route 24 through Morristown (signs may read 24/124). Look for the entrance to Lewis Morris Park on the left and the Patriots' Path parking area on the right, about 3.5 miles west of I-287.

West Essex Rail Trail

Considering its urban location, this trail is a jewel in the rough, offering what might be the longest legal off-road cycling opportunity in the Essex-Hudson County area.

You won't find technical singletrack or monster hill climbs here, but the trail does offer some relief from traffic and noise pollution.

This is an out-and-back route on one of New Jersey's least known and only moderately used rail trails. Although located in the heavily urbanized part of the state, the trail passes through sections of woodland, providing a short escape from the surrounding congestion.

Unfortunately, the most scenic section of the trail is currently in disrepair. Refer to the Pompton Avenue / Community Park area inset on the trail map for the location of the trestle that once carried heavy loads over the Peckman River. Because the trestle is currently in poor condition, using it to cross the river is highly discouraged. Refer to the map inset to bypass this area.

A picturesque view of the river is available at the point where you leave Community Park crossing a small bridge connecting to Little Falls Road.

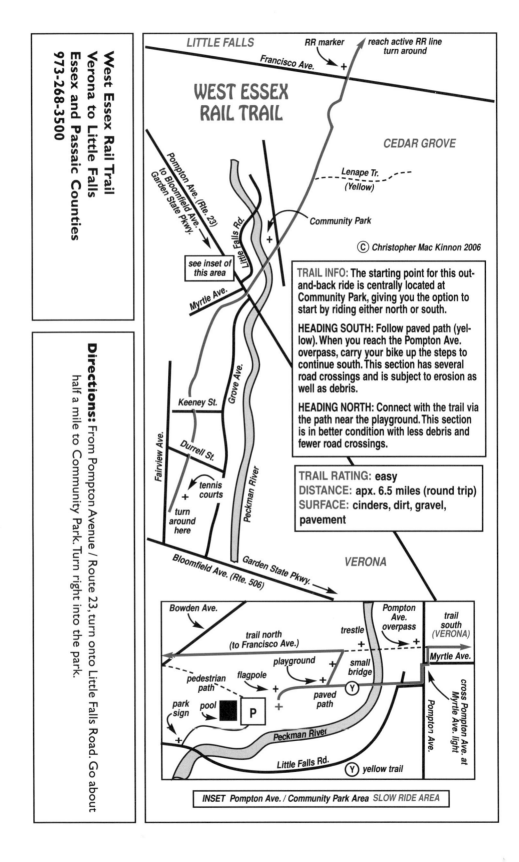

West Essex Rail Trail
Verona to Little Falls
Essex and Passaic Counties
973-268-3500

Directions: From Pompton Avenue / Route 23, turn onto Little Falls Road. Go about half a mile to Community Park. Turn right into the park.

LITTLE FALLS
RR marker
reach active RR line turn around
Francisco Ave.

WEST ESSEX
RAIL TRAIL

CEDAR GROVE

Pompton Ave. (Rte. 23)
to Bloomfield Ave. /
Garden State Pkwy.

Little Falls Rd.

Lenape Tr. (Yellow)

Community Park

© Christopher Mac Kinnon 2006

see inset of this area

Myrtle Ave.

TRAIL INFO: The starting point for this out-and-back ride is centrally located at Community Park, giving you the option to start by riding either north or south.

HEADING SOUTH: Follow paved path (yellow). When you reach the Pompton Ave. overpass, carry your bike up the steps to continue south. This section has several road crossings and is subject to erosion as well as debris.

HEADING NORTH: Connect with the trail via the path near the playground. This section is in better condition with less debris and fewer road crossings.

Grove Ave.

Keeney St.

Fairview Ave.

Durrell St.

tennis courts

turn around here

Peckman River

TRAIL RATING: easy
DISTANCE: apx. 6.5 miles (round trip)
SURFACE: cinders, dirt, gravel, pavement

Bloomfield Ave. (Rte. 506)

Garden State Pkwy.

VERONA

Bowden Ave.

trail north (to Francisco Ave.)

trestle

Pompton Ave. overpass

trail south (VERONA)

Myrtle Ave.

pedestrian path

flagpole

playground

small bridge

Y

park sign

pool

P

paved path

Pompton Ave.

cross Pompton Ave. at Myrtle Ave. light

Peckman River

Little Falls Rd.

Y yellow trail

INSET Pompton Ave. / Community Park Area SLOW RIDE AREA

Sign at the Califon Museum

Columbia Trail
Lockwood Gorge

As the South Branch of the Raritan River winds its way through Hunterdon County, its demeanor changes, gradually at first, then abruptly south of the village of Califon. Rolling farmland and gently sloping banks give way to a rugged landscape as you enter the Ken Lockwood Gorge, aptly named after an environmental visionary who was instrumental in preserving the area.

For the next 2 miles, the landscape is characterized by jagged rock outcroppings and steep forested walls populated by evergreens. The once-placid Raritan changes its temperament as well as it rushes noisily over and around rocks and boulders of varying sizes and shapes. This section of the river, protected as part of the Ken Lockwood Gorge Wildlife Management Area, is treasured as one of the state's prime fly-fishing areas.

(See page 21 for more information on the WMA system, including the New Jersey Fish and Wildlife Division's official policies on riding in these areas.)

This route takes you beside the river and through the gorge via Raritan River Road, as well as above the gorge via the Columbia Rail Trail. The combination of a tree-shaded trail and the opportunity to enjoy the cooling effects of the river make this an ideal destination for a leisurely ride on a hot summer day.

An old iron bridge and the railroad station that now serves as the Califon Museum add both atmosphere and history to the village of Califon. The Califon Museum (see map for location), built in 1875, houses a collection of railroad memorabilia and Americana and is open from 1 to 3 P.M. on the first and third Sundays of the month between May and December.

Parking is available in High Bridge at the Borough Commons municipal lot or along the trail itself off Mill Street (see map insert for locations).

The route initially begins as an unmaintained dirt road between Main Street and Mill Street and soon goes under a bridge. After passing several houses, the trail narrows and parallels the river, eventually crossing it.

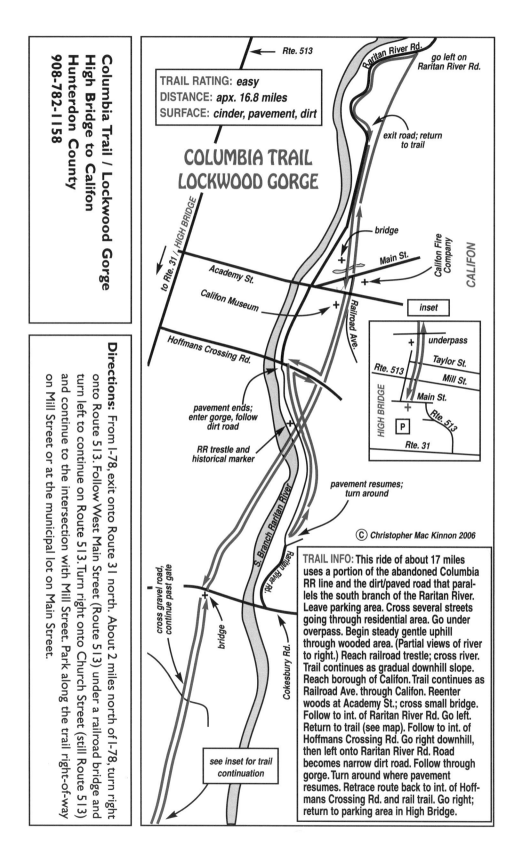

Columbia Trail / Lockwood Gorge
High Bridge to Califon
Hunterdon County
908-782-1158

TRAIL RATING: *easy*
DISTANCE: *apx. 16.8 miles*
SURFACE: *cinder, pavement, dirt*

COLUMBIA TRAIL
LOCKWOOD GORGE

Rte. 513

go left on
Raritan River Rd.

Raritan River Rd.

exit road; return
to trail

to Rte. 31 / HIGH BRIDGE

bridge

Academy St.

Califon Museum

Main St.

Califon Fire
Company

CALIFON

Railroad Ave.

Hoffmans Crossing Rd.

inset

underpass

Taylor St.

Rte. 513

Mill St.

Main St.

HIGH BRIDGE

P

Rte. 513

Rte. 31

pavement ends;
enter gorge, follow
dirt road

RR trestle and
historical marker

pavement resumes;
turn around

© *Christopher Mac Kinnon 2006*

cross gravel road,
continue past gate

bridge

S. Branch Raritan River

Raritan River Rd.

Cokesbury Rd.

see inset for trail
continuation

Directions: From I-78, exit onto Route 31 north. About 2 miles north of I-78, turn right onto Route 513. Follow West Main Street (Route 513) under a railroad bridge and turn left to continue on Route 513. Turn right onto Church Street (still Route 513) and continue to the intersection with Mill Street. Park along the trail right-of-way on Mill Street or at the municipal lot on Main Street.

TRAIL INFO: This ride of about 17 miles uses a portion of the abandoned Columbia RR line and the dirt/paved road that parallels the south branch of the Raritan River. Leave parking area. Cross several streets going through residential area. Go under overpass. Begin steady gentle uphill through wooded area. (Partial views of river to right.) Reach railroad trestle; cross river. Trail continues as gradual downhill slope. Reach borough of Califon. Trail continues as Railroad Ave. through Califon. Reenter woods at Academy St.; cross small bridge. Follow to int. of Raritan River Rd. Go left. Return to trail (see map). Follow to int. of Hoffmans Crossing Rd. Go right downhill, then left onto Raritan River Rd. Road becomes narrow dirt road. Follow through gorge. Turn around where pavement resumes. Retrace route back to int. of Hoffmans Crossing Rd. and rail trail. Go right; return to parking area in High Bridge.

Voorhees State Park

The beginnings of Voorhees State Park can be traced back to 1929, when Foster M. Voorhees, a former governor of New Jersey, donated his 325-acre farm to the people of the state. Succeeding land acquisitions have increased the size of the park to its present 640 acres.

Trails, shelters, and picnic sites were constructed during the 1930s under the Civilian Conservation Corps. Since that time, Voorhees has grown into a multi-use facility. In addition to mountain biking, fishing, hunting, and hiking are among the activities available at the park. Trails here are multi-use except for the Cross Park Trail, which is restricted to foot travel only. The Highland Trail, which is not indicated on the park trail map, also runs through the park. This is a relatively new trail connecting parks, forests, and public open spaces in northern New Jersey and southern New York State. It is advisable to check at the park office regarding access to this trail.

One of the outstanding features of the park is the observatory located off Hill Acres Road (see the map for location). The 28-inch reflector telescope is one of the largest privately owned telescopes in the state. The New Jersey Astronomical Association offers various programs throughout the year. For information, call 908-638-8500.

This loop ride through the park uses wide doubletrack trails, primitive park roads, paved road, and a short stretch of singletrack on the section of trail between the observatory and the scenic overlook. Keep an eye out for hikers who may be using this route to walk from the overlook area to the observatory.

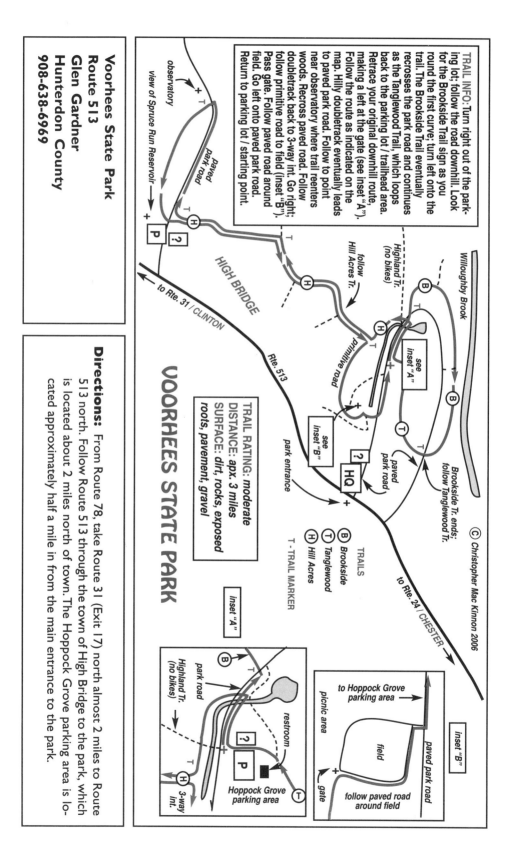

Voorhees State Park
Route 513
Glen Gardner
Hunterdon County
908-638-6969

TRAIL INFO: Turn right out of the parking lot; follow the road downhill. Look for the Brookside Trail sign as you round the first curve; turn left onto the trail. The Brookside Trail eventually recrosses the park road and continues as the Tanglewood Trail, which loops back to the parking lot / trailhead area. Retrace your original downhill route, making a left at the gate (see inset "A"). Follow the route as indicated on the map. Hilly doubletrack eventually leads to paved park road. Follow to point near observatory where trail reenters woods. Follow paved road. Follow doubletrack back to 3-way int. Go right; Pass gate. Follow paved road around field. Go left onto paved park road. Return to parking lot / starting point.

view of Spruce Run Reservoir

observatory

paved park road

HIGH BRIDGE

to Rte. 31 / CLINTON

Rte. 513

follow Hill Acres Tr.

Highland Tr. (no bikes)

primitive road

Willoughby Brook

Brookside Tr. ends; follow Tanglewood Tr.

see inset "A"

see inset "B"

paved park road

park entrance

© Christopher Mac Kinnon 2006

to Rte. 24 / CHESTER

VOORHEES STATE PARK

TRAIL RATING: *moderate*
DISTANCE: *apx. 3 miles*
SURFACE: *dirt, rocks, exposed roots, pavement, gravel*

TRAILS
Ⓑ *Brookside*
Ⓣ *Tanglewood*
Ⓗ *Hill Acres*

T - TRAIL MARKER

HQ

inset "A"

Highland Tr. (no bikes)

park road

restroom

Hoppock Grove parking area

3-way int.

inset "B"

to Hoppock Grove parking area

picnic area

field

gate

paved park road

follow paved road around field

Directions: From Route 78, take Route 31 (Exit 17) north almost 2 miles to Route 513 north. Follow Route 513 through the town of High Bridge to the park, which is located about 2 miles north of town. The Hoppock Grove parking area is located approximately half a mile in from the main entrance to the park.

Round Valley Recreation Area

Your first impression of the Round Valley Recreation Area will be of size. Large by New Jersey standards, the reservoir and horseshoe-shaped Cushetunk Mountain dwarf many of the other ride locations in this book. Round Valley is big not only in physical size (with a combined 7,300-plus acres) but psychologically as well, perhaps because of the configuration of the surrounding mountains and expanse of pristine water.

Regarded as the mecca of New Jersey mountain biking by some, its reputation is well deserved. You can expect both conditioning and bike-handling skills to be tested here.

This out-and-back route starts off innocently enough as a relatively tame trail heading away from the parking lot. It doesn't really begin to reveal its true identity until about 1.5 miles into the ride. After reaching a chain-link fence, the trail descends steeply, the first of many steep climbs and descents. From this point on, you can expect to encounter long and demanding ascents and descents, as well as heavily eroded sections of trail and rocks the size of bowling balls.

An equipment check is a must at Round Valley. Stock up on extra tubes, patches, etc. before starting out. This is a punishing ride where self-reliance is the rule. For emergency purposes there's a telephone located at the beach area next to a small cluster of buildings at approximately 5.6 miles into the route (see trail map).

Round Valley is a multi-use recreation area. Although it serves primarily as a water source holding in excess of 50 billion gallons, it is also highly valued by fisherman, boaters, and hikers. Cyclists should ride slowly in the area near the wilderness parking area. This section of the trail is heavily used by pedestrians who want to view the reservoir. The nearby Pine Tree Trail is off limits to bikes. Stay on the designated route (the Cushetunk Trail) and watch for posted private-property signs to the right as you ride the prescribed route. This trail is marked with various symbols including a horseshoe, footprint, and arrow, as shown in the trail sign pictured on page 61.

ROUND VALLEY RECREATION AREA

LEBANON

← Rte. 78 / CLINTON

← Rte. 22 / SOMERVILLE →

Exit 20 →

Lebanon-Stanton Rd. (Rte. 629)

CLINTON TWP.

TRAIL INFO: This 14-mile out-and-back ride starts at the rear of the wilderness camping parking lot. The Cushetunk Trail is well marked, using a system of round yellow discs along with a green footprint on a yellow backround. This ride offers the off-road enthuiast some of the most challenging terrain in the Garden State. Trails range from wide doubletrack to highly technical singletrack. Trail surfaces vary from packed dirt and gravel to large rocks and exposed roots. After a heavy rain, the first third of the trail is likely to be extremely muddy (and perhaps best avoided in the interest of preventing soil erosion).

BRING YOUR TOOL KIT AND AN EXTRA TUBE. THERE ARE NO FACILITIES ALONG THE ROUTE. THE GRAVEL ROAD THROUGH THE WILDERNESS AREA MAY BE CLOSED TO BIKES. INQUIRE AT THE PARK OFFICE REGARDING ACCESS TO THIS AREA.

Round Valley Recreation Area
Route 629 (Lebanon-Stanton Road)
Lebanon
Hunterdon County
908-236-6355

Directions: Take I-78 to Exit 20 and follow signs to Round Valley Recreation Area via Route 22, parking at the entrance off Route 629 (Lebanon-Stanton Road).

park road

to Rte. 31 ←

park bldg.;
turn left

trail/wilderness
sign

wilderness area begins;
follow trail uphill at
4-way int.

Cushetunk Trail

see inset

Inset

Round Valley
Reservoir

park office
and tollbooth

ent. road

Rte. 629

south parking lot

P

Cushetunk Trail

TRAIL RATING: difficult
DISTANCE: apx. 14 miles
round trip
SURFACE: dirt, gravel, roots

at bottom of long downhill,
go right at wood posts

WILDERNESS AREA
NO BIKES

telephone

Cushetunk Trail

Cushetunk Mountain 834'

STANTON

gravel road

distinct 3-way int.;
go straight past
woodposts

very steep trail
to right

trail reaches distinct 4-way int.;
turn around and return via
the same route

Cushetunk Trail sign

Capoolong Creek location sign

Capoolong Creek Wildlife Management Area

Just over 2 feet deep and perhaps 20 feet wide in spots, Capoolong Creek meanders through central Hunterdon County before emptying into the South Branch of the Raritan River. An aerial view would show it as a pretty ribbon winding through several rural communities.

Running along the creek from Pittstown to Landsdowne is a long, narrow wildlife management zone marked with numerous posted signs. The Capoolong Creek Wildlife Management Area, one of 126 WMAs in New Jersey, serves as a buffer zone to development. (See page 21 for more information on the WMA system, including the New Jersey Fish and Wildlife Division's official policies on riding in these areas.)

Not as well known as neighboring Lockwood Gorge, another WMA, it nonetheless is also popular with fishermen—and a satisfying destination for the casual rider.

The wildlife management area encompasses what was once a branch of the Lehigh Valley Railroad, a fact that is evidenced by lingering railroad bridges, embedded ties, and even a train station, now in disrepair. The rail trail is a little over 3 miles long, relatively flat, and quite lovely as it winds along beside the creek. This is not a challenging ride by any means, but the scenery makes it worth the effort.

As a curiosity, the name Capoolong has several variant spellings and is sometimes seen as Cakepoulin on various maps and road signs.

CAPOOLONG CREEK WILDLIFE MANAGEMENT AREA

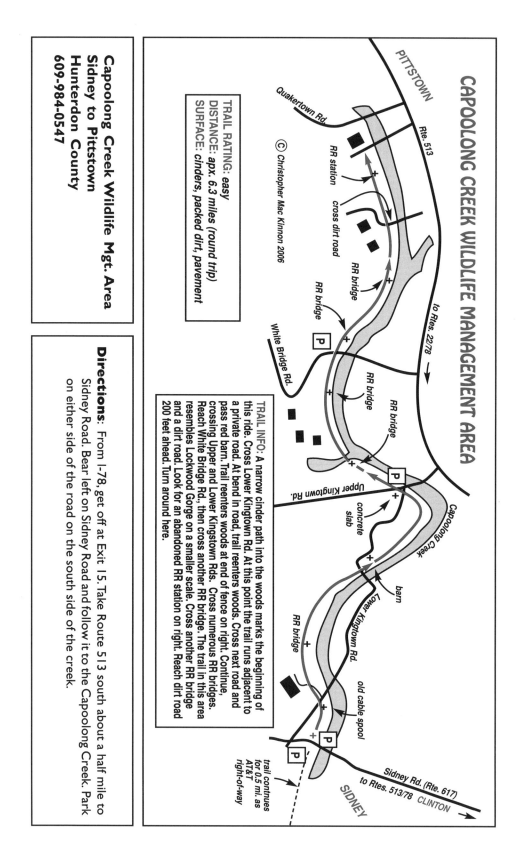

© Christopher Mac Kinnon 2006

TRAIL RATING: *easy*
DISTANCE: *apx. 6.3 miles (round trip)*
SURFACE: *cinders, packed dirt, pavement*

TRAIL INFO: A narrow cinder path into the woods marks the beginning of this ride. Cross Lower Kingtown Rd. At this point the trail runs adjacent to a private road. At bend in road, trail reenters woods at end of fence on right. Cross next road and pass red barn. Trail reenters woods at end of fence on right. Continue, crossing Upper and Lower Kingtown Rds. Cross numerous RR bridges. Reach White Bridge Rd., then cross another RR bridge. The trail in this area resembles Lockwood Gorge on a smaller scale. Cross another RR bridge and a dirt road. Look for an abandoned RR station on right. Reach dirt road 200 feet ahead. Turn around here.

Capoolong Creek Wildlife Mgt. Area
Sidney to Pittstown
Hunterdon County
609-984-0547

Directions: From I-78, get off at Exit 15. Take Route 513 south about a half mile to Sidney Road. Bear left on Sidney Road and follow it to the Capoolong Creek. Park on either side of the road on the south side of the creek.

Delaware and Raritan Feeder Canal

The Delaware and Raritan Feeder Canal was originally constructed to provide water to the main canal (see page 71). Its diverse scenery, quaint crossroads, and agreeable trail surface make it ideal even for casual cyclists. It runs through the heart of an area that is immensely popular with tourists, and you'll find a series of interesting towns and worthwhile detours along the way.

Until a few years ago, the multi-use path beside the feeder canal was divided into two distinct sections. One ran from just north of Trenton to Lambertville, the other from just north of Lambertville to Frenchtown. Happily, however, the two sections have been joined, so it is now possible to ride the entire path straight through. For most cyclists interested in this type of ride, however, a jaunt covering part of the trail will suffice for a day's outing.

The Delaware Canal on the Pennsylvania side of the Delaware River also has a bikeable towpath, but it suffered major damage during Delaware River flooding in 2005. (The path on the New Jersey side had some damage, too, but it has been repaired.) Cyclists should check the Delaware Canal State Park web site at **http://www.dcnr.state.pa.us/stateparks/parks/ delawarecanal.aspx** to see what areas are open before planning to ride on the Pennsylvania side.

The **Delaware and Raritan Feeder Canal (North)** map shows the route starting at Prallsville Mills, north of Stockton on Route 29. You might want to look through the restored mill and surrounding buildings and grounds during your visit. No longer operating as a working mill, this 19th-century building is often host to art shows, concerts, and private parties.

The atmosphere along this stretch of the canal is markedly different from the southern section. The feeling of being in the woods is strong here. Development is minimal along this portion of Route 29, and traffic is considerably lighter than around Lambertville and Washington Crossing. The wide shoulder along the road provides another safe alternate route for your return trip.

Include a short side trip to Bull's Island if time allows. The feeder canal begins at the northern tip of the island. Follow the paved road past the park headquarters (left turn from the towpath if you're riding north) to the narrow pedestrian bridge that crosses the river. On the Pennsylvania side is the quaint village of Lumberville. North of Bull's Island, canal views are replaced by glimpses of the river to the left and ever-increasing rock outcroppings accompanied by soaring hawks to the right.

Frenchtown is an attractive riverside community where you can grab a bite to eat, relax, and enjoy the sights along the river before starting back.

The route detailed in the **Delaware and Raritan Feeder Canal (South)** map begins at New Jersey's Washington Crossing State Park, located at the intersection of Route 546 and River Road near the bridge across the Delaware River. The towns of Washington Crossing (there are two by that name, one in New Jersey and the other in Pennsylvania) are easily accessible from the trailhead parking area. If you take the bridge across the river to Washington Crossing, Pa., you'll find a collection of istoric buildings housing Revolutionary War memorabilia immediately to your right. Included are replicas of the boats used by George Washington during his fateful river crossing on Christmas night in 1776.

To reach the main part of New Jersey's Washington Crossing State Park, walk your bike across the pedestrian overpass next to the trailhead. If time allows, include at least a visit to the park visitor center and Continental Lane. Another detour worth considering is the scenic riverside village of Titusville, shown on the map as an alternate return route.

In Lambertville, you can stop for refreshments or to visit some of the town's many antique shops, or venture across the river to New Hope. Art galleries, antiquing, fine dining, and everything but the ordinary only begins to describe a side trip to New Hope.

Old millstone along the Delaware and Raritan Feeder Canal

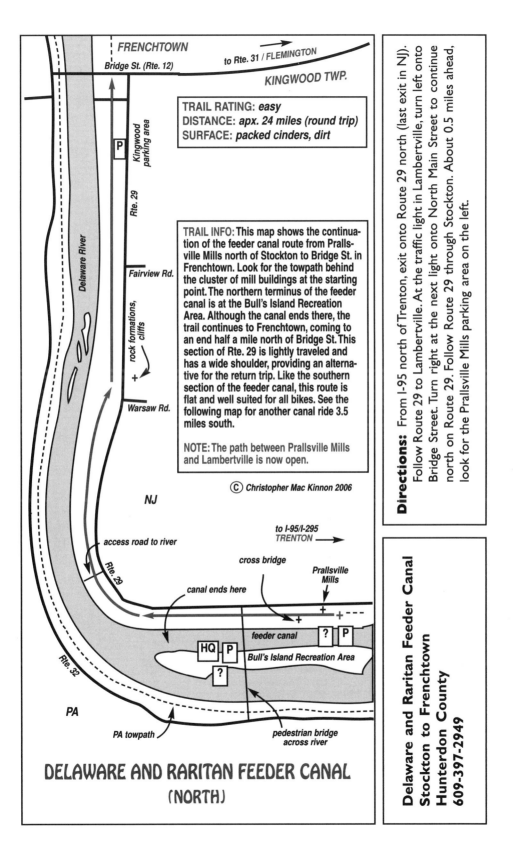

FRENCHTOWN
Bridge St. (Rte. 12)
to Rte. 31 / FLEMINGTON
KINGWOOD TWP.

Kingwood parking area
Rte. 29
Delaware River
Fairview Rd.
rock formations, cliffs
Warsaw Rd.

TRAIL RATING: *easy*
DISTANCE: *apx. 24 miles (round trip)*
SURFACE: *packed cinders, dirt*

TRAIL INFO: This map shows the continuation of the feeder canal route from Prallsville Mills north of Stockton to Bridge St. in Frenchtown. Look for the towpath behind the cluster of mill buildings at the starting point. The northern terminus of the feeder canal is at the Bull's Island Recreation Area. Although the canal ends there, the trail continues to Frenchtown, coming to an end half a mile north of Bridge St. This section of Rte. 29 is lightly traveled and has a wide shoulder, providing an alternative for the return trip. Like the southern section of the feeder canal, this route is flat and well suited for all bikes. See the following map for another canal ride 3.5 miles south.

NOTE: The path between Prallsville Mills and Lambertville is now open.

© *Christopher Mac Kinnon 2006*

NJ

access road to river
Rte. 29
Rte. 32
PA

to I-95/I-295
TRENTON →

cross bridge
Prallsville Mills
canal ends here
feeder canal
HQ P
?
Bull's Island Recreation Area
? P

PA towpath
pedestrian bridge across river

DELAWARE AND RARITAN FEEDER CANAL
(NORTH)

Directions: From I-95 north of Trenton, exit onto Route 29 north (last exit in NJ). Follow Route 29 to Lambertville. At the traffic light in Lambertville, turn left onto Bridge Street. Turn right at the next light onto North Main Street to continue north on Route 29. Follow Route 29 through Stockton. About 0.5 miles ahead, look for the Prallsville Mills parking area on the left.

Delaware and Raritan Feeder Canal
Stockton to Frenchtown
Hunterdon County
609-397-2949

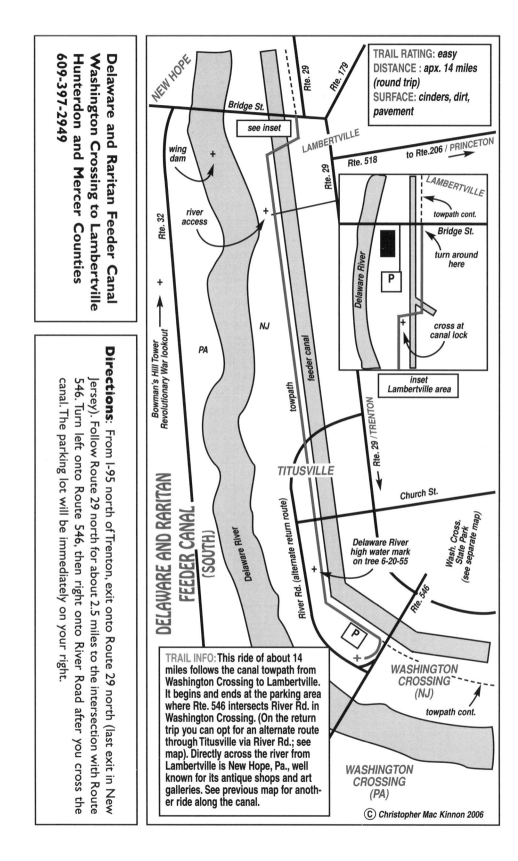

Delaware and Raritan Feeder Canal

Washington Crossing to Lambertville

Hunterdon and Mercer Counties

609-397-2949

Directions: From I-95 north of Trenton, exit onto Route 29 north (last exit in New Jersey). Follow Route 29 north for about 2.5 miles to the intersection with Route 546. Turn left onto Route 546, then right onto River Road after you cross the canal. The parking lot will be immediately on your right.

TRAIL RATING: *easy*
DISTANCE : *apx. 14 miles (round trip)*
SURFACE: *cinders, dirt, pavement*

NEW HOPE

Bridge St.

see inset

Rte. 29

Rte. 179

LAMBERTVILLE

to Rte. 206 / PRINCETON

Rte. 29

Rte. 518

wing dam

river access

Rte. 32

Bowman's Hill Tower
Revolutionary War lookout →

PA

NJ

feeder canal

towpath

LAMBERTVILLE

towpath cont.

Bridge St.

turn around here

P

Delaware River

cross at canal lock

inset Lambertville area

Rte. 29 / TRENTON

TITUSVILLE

Church St.

DELAWARE AND RARITAN FEEDER CANAL (SOUTH)

Delaware River

River Rd. (alternate return route)

Delaware River high water mark on tree 6-20-55

Wash. Cross. State Park (see separate map)

Rte. 546

P

WASHINGTON CROSSING (NJ)

towpath cont.

WASHINGTON CROSSING (PA)

TRAIL INFO: This ride of about 14 miles follows the canal towpath from Washington Crossing to Lambertville. It begins and ends at the parking area where Rte. 546 intersects River Rd. in Washington Crossing. (On the return trip you can opt for an alternate route through Titusville via River Rd.; see map). Directly across the river from Lambertville is New Hope, Pa., well known for its antique shops and art galleries. See previous map for another ride along the canal.

© Christopher Mac Kinnon 2006

Washington Valley County Park

Washington Valley is not the same kind of destination as High Point State Park or Round Valley Reservoir, with their obvious attractions and family-oriented recreational facilities. Instead, you could think of it as those woods across the street where you used to play … only much bigger!

Washington Valley County Park, also known as White Rocks or Chimney Rock and shown on some county maps as the Watchung Reservation, has much to offer the off-road enthusiast. Although located in Central Jersey, its trails are more like those found in the northern part of the state. The park includes about 2,000 acres with an extensive network of trails to explore, many of which are in the form of rocky, steep, twisting, unforgiving singletrack. This secluded gem is a prime area for mountain biking in New Jersey and, hopefully, development and restrictions will be kept to a minimum in the future.

Except for the posted Somerset County parks signs loosely defining the perimeter of the park, there is little at Washington Valley to indicate county ownership. As you explore the network of singletrack trails, dirt paths, and gravel roads that combine to make up the route, you might get the feeling that this area is an extension of the many backyards that are adjacent to the trail. Diplomacy and trail etiquette are highly recommended here! Locals seem to be very protective of the area. Be a positive representative for your sport; if you are not sure about area boundaries, ask or select an alternate route.

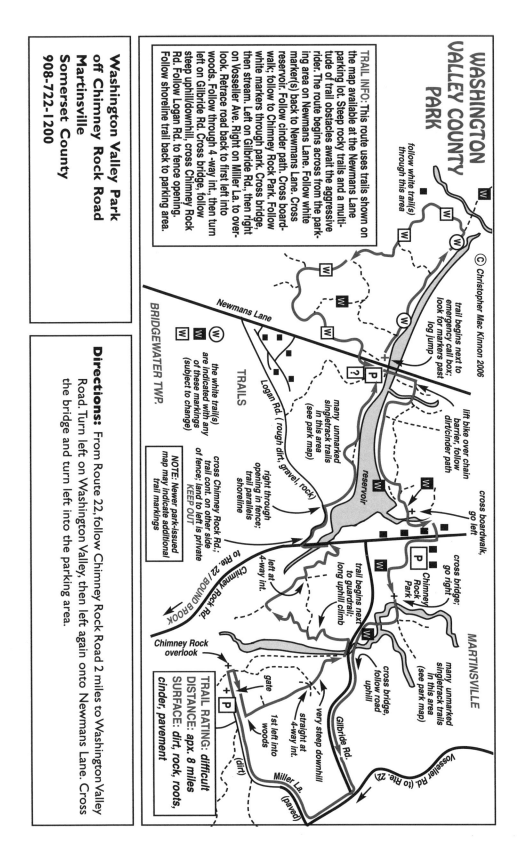

WASHINGTON VALLEY COUNTY PARK

© Christopher Mac Kinnon 2006

TRAIL INFO: This route uses trails shown on the map available at the Newmans Lane parking lot. Steep rocky trails and a multitude of trail obstacles await the aggressive rider. The route begins across from the parking area on Newmans Lane. Follow white marker(s) back to Newmans Lane. Cross reservoir. Follow cinder path. Cross boardwalk; follow to Chimney Rock Park. Follow white markers through park. Cross board-walk; follow to Chimney Rock Park. Follow white markers through park. Cross bridge, then stream. Left on Gilbride Rd., then right on Gilbride Rd. to overlook. Retrace road back to first left into woods. Follow 4-way int., then turn left on Gilbride Rd. Cross bridge, follow steep uphill/downhill, cross Chimney Rock Rd. Follow Logan Rd. to fence opening. Follow shoreline trail back to parking area.

follow white trail(s) through this area

trail begins next to emergency call box; look for markers past log jump

lift bike over chain barrier, follow dirt/cinder path

Newmans Lane

BRIDGEWATER TWP.

TRAILS

Logan Rd. (rough dirt, gravel, rock)

the white trail(s) are indicated with any of these markings (subject to change)

many unmarked singletrack trails in this area (see park map)

reservoir

cross boardwalk, go left

cross bridge; go left

NOTE: Newer park-issued map may indicate additional trail markings

cross Chimney Rock Rd.; trail cont. on other side of fence; land to left is private KEEP OUT

right through opening in fence; trail parallels shoreline

left at 4-way int.

Chimney Rock Rd. to Rte. 22 / BOUND BROOK

trail begins next; long uphill climb

cross bridge; go right

Chimney Rock Park

MARTINSVILLE

many unmarked singletrack trails in this area (see park map)

Chimney Rock overlook

gate

cross bridge, follow road uphill

very steep downhill

straight at 4-way int.

Gilbride Rd.

Vosseler Rd. (to Rte. 22)

1st left into woods

Miller La. (paved)

(dirt)

Washington Valley Rd. (to Rte. 22)

TRAIL RATING: difficult
DISTANCE: apx. 8 miles
SURFACE: dirt, rock, roots, cinder, pavement

**Washington Valley Park
off Chimney Rock Road
Martinsville
Somerset County
908-722-1200**

Directions: From Route 22, follow Chimney Rock Road 2 miles to Washington Valley Road. Turn left on Washington Valley, then left again onto Newmans Lane. Cross the bridge and turn left into the parking area.

Delaware and Raritan Canal

Words such as placid, tranquil, and relaxing only begin to describe the atmosphere that is pervasive along the Delaware and Raritan Canal.

The canal is living testimony to the thousands of Irish immigrants who built it by hand between 1830 and 1834. When completed, it linked Bordentown in the south with New Brunswick to the north and served as an artery for transportation before the development of a widespread railroad system. Far removed now from its historic past, the Delaware and Raritan Canal today meets the needs of the surrounding area as a multi-use recreational facility suitable for canoeing, hiking, biking, fishing, and horseback riding. It also serves as a source of drinking water.

Although the mule-drawn barges are long gone, the towpath they trod still exists, and for much of its length it has been preserved as a New Jersey state park. It stands as a monument to historical foresight and preservation. This 35-mile greenway offers the longest continuous off-road opportunity for the New Jersey cyclist. With minimal interruptions you can ride from Alexander Road in Princeton to just south of the Route 18 bridge across the Raritan River in New Brunswick.

On its way, the canal passes through a number of small towns and villages, including Princeton, Griggstown, and Kingston. You can also find evidence of a once-vibrant trade route along the towpath. Historic buildings are located along the canal in Kingston, Griggstown, and Blackwells Mills, and there are several locks that were used to facilitate barge movement along the route. Look for the 22-mile marker north of Route 518 (see map for location). This was the halfway point of the original canal as it ran from Trenton to New Brunswick.

Canoe rentals are available in Griggstown and Princeton. Griggstown is also home to the canal museum, located just to the left of the towpath as you head north (see map).

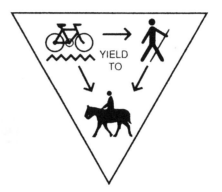

Trail etiquette

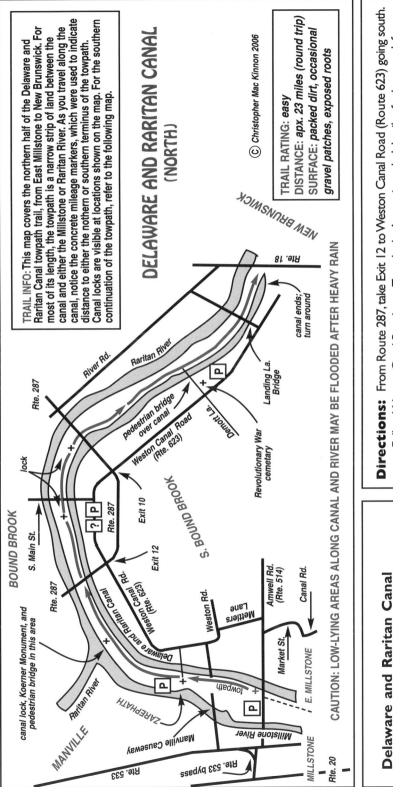

DELAWARE AND RARITAN CANAL
(NORTH)

TRAIL INFO: This map covers the northern half of the Delaware and Raritan Canal towpath trail, from East Millstone to New Brunswick. For most of its length, the towpath is a narrow strip of land between the canal and either the Millstone or Raritan River. As you travel along the canal, notice the concrete mileage markers, which were used to indicate distance to either the northern or southern terminus of the towpath. Canal locks are visible at locations shown on the map. For the southern continuation of the towpath, refer to the following map.

© Christopher Mac Kinnon 2006

TRAIL RATING: *easy*
DISTANCE: *apx. 23 miles (round trip)*
SURFACE: *packed dirt, occasional gravel patches, exposed roots*

CAUTION: LOW-LYING AREAS ALONG CANAL AND RIVER MAY BE FLOODED AFTER HEAVY RAIN

Directions: From Route 287, take Exit 12 to Weston Canal Road (Route 623) going south. Follow Weston Canal Road past Zarephath. Approximately 1.1 miles farther, turn left onto Weston Road before crossing the canal (there's an old white house on the corner). Follow Weston Road to Metlers Lane. Turn right onto Metlers. Pass Colonial Park. Turn right onto Amwell Road (Route 514). Parking is on the right immediately after you cross the canal.

Delaware and Raritan Canal
East Millstone to New Brunswick
Somerset and Middlesex Counties
609-924-5705

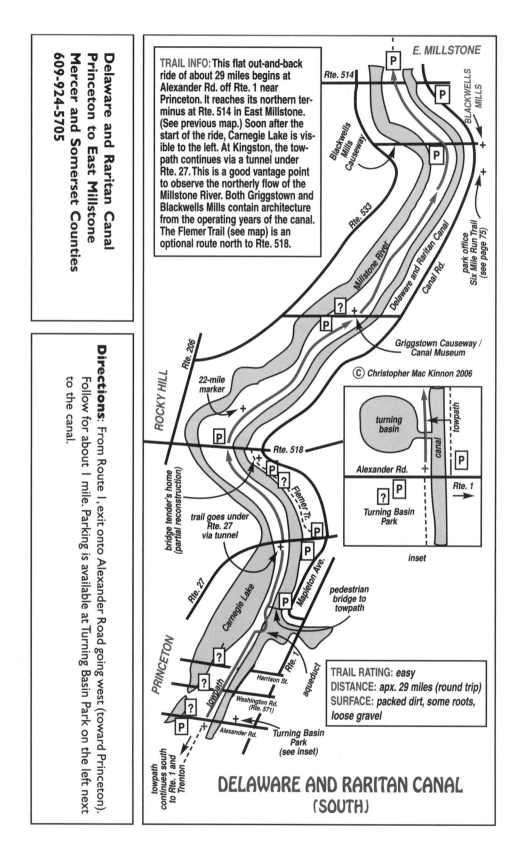

Delaware and Raritan Canal
Princeton to East Millstone
Mercer and Somerset Counties
609-924-5705

Directions: From Route 1, exit onto Alexander Road going west (toward Princeton). Follow for about 1 mile. Parking is available at Turning Basin Park on the left next to the canal.

TRAIL INFO: This flat out-and-back ride of about 29 miles begins at Alexander Rd. off Rte. 1 near Princeton. It reaches its northern terminus at Rte. 514 in East Millstone. (See previous map.) Soon after the start of the ride, Carnegie Lake is visible to the left. At Kingston, the towpath continues via a tunnel under Rte. 27. This is a good vantage point to observe the northerly flow of the Millstone River. Both Griggstown and Blackwells Mills contain architecture from the operating years of the canal. The Flemer Trail (see map) is an optional route north to Rte. 518.

E. MILLSTONE

Rte. 514

BLACKWELLS MILLS

Blackwells Mills Causeway

Rte. 533

Millstone River

Delaware and Raritan Canal Rd.

park office
Six Mile Run Trail
(see page 75)

Griggstown Causeway /
Canal Museum

© Christopher Mac Kinnon 2006

Rte. 206

ROCKY HILL

22-mile marker

Rte. 518

bridge tender's home (partial reconstruction)

trail goes under Rte. 27 via tunnel

Flemer Tr.

Rte. 27

Carnegie Lake

Mapleton Ave.

pedestrian bridge to towpath

PRINCETON

towpath

Harrison St.

Rte. 1

Washington Rd. (Rte. 571)

Alexander Rd.

aqueduct

Turning Basin Park (see inset)

towpath continues south to Rte. 1 and Trenton

inset

turning basin

towpath

canal

Alexander Rd.

Turning Basin Park

Rte. 1

TRAIL RATING: *easy*
DISTANCE: *apx. 29 miles (round trip)*
SURFACE: *packed dirt, some roots, loose gravel*

DELAWARE AND RARITAN CANAL
(SOUTH)

Six Mile Run Reservoir

The first thing you'll probably ask yourself as you start this ride is "where's the reservoir?"

The answer is "right here" and "there really isn't one ... yet."

Confusing? Not really. According to the park brochure, development of this project won't begin until around the year 2020, giving cyclists ample time to explore this hidden off-road resource in central New Jersey.

In an earlier era, the area was cultivated by Dutch farmers who had migrated from Long Island, and many barns here date back to this time. Preserved today as a multi-use recreation area (seasonal bow hunting is permitted) and watershed, it stands as a visual reminder of an agrarian landscape once common in the Raritan Valley area.

In contrast to the nearby Delaware and Raritan Canal towpath, which is quite flat, this route uses rolling doubletrack (watch out for the groundhog holes!) as well as narrow singletrack with occasional trail obstacles and possible shallow water crossings.

Perhaps the word "potential" best describes Six Mile Run. Although the facility is sizable at 3,000 acres, only sections of this site are now open to the public. Cyclists should not cross Six Mile Run, as the area south of the creek is currently closed to bikes. This may or may not change at some future date, according to park personnel, who also report that both trail designations and trail routes are subject to change pending further assessment of activity requirements and environmental impact. Because of this, it would be a good idea to inquire at the park office regarding current trail conditions and updates before starting your ride.

The route shown on this map uses the yellow-blazed singletrack trail, which runs adjacent to Six Mile Run, and a section of the blue-blazed North Pilot Trail. This short ride is intended to be an introduction to this area rather than an attempt at a comprehensive tour through the entire site. For information on the nearby towpath trail and roads in the area, refer to the Delaware and Raritan Canal (South) map.

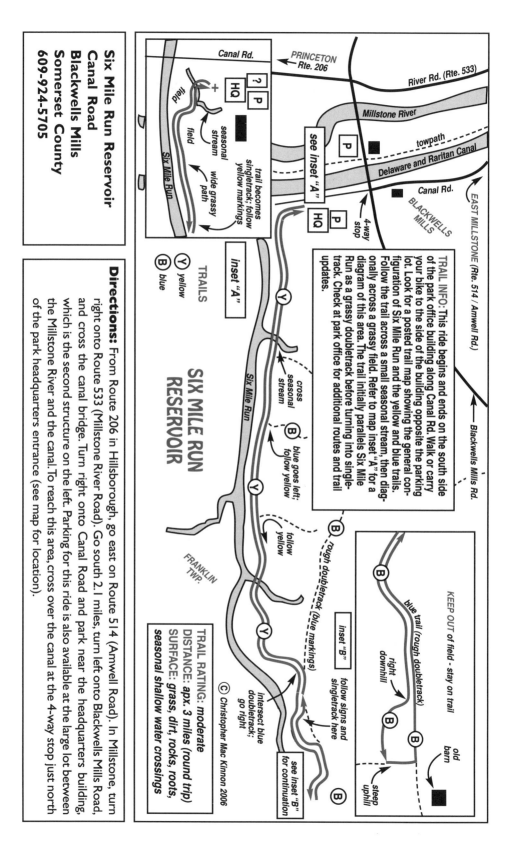

Six Mile Run Reservoir
Canal Road
Blackwells Mills
Somerset County
609-924-5705

Directions: From Route 206 in Hillsborough, go east on Route 514 (Amwell Road). In Millstone, turn right onto Route 533 (Millstone River Road). Go south 2.1 miles, turn left onto Blackwells Mills Road, and cross the canal bridge. Turn right onto Canal Road and park near the headquarters building, which is the second structure on the left. Parking for this ride is also available at the large lot between the Millstone River and the canal. To reach this area, cross over the canal at the 4-way stop just north of the park headquarters entrance (see map for location).

PRINCETON
Rte. 206

Canal Rd.

River Rd. (Rte. 533)

Millstone River

towpath

Delaware and Raritan Canal

Canal Rd.

BLACKWELLS MILLS

EAST MILLSTONE (Rte. 514 / Amwell Rd.)

Blackwells Mills Rd.

see inset "A"

4-way stop

HQ

P

TRAIL INFO: This ride begins and ends on the south side of the park office building along Canal Rd. Walk or carry your bike to the side of the building opposite the parking lot. Look for a posted trail map showing the general configuration of Six Mile Run and the yellow and blue trails. Follow the trail across a small seasonal stream, then diagonally across a grassy field. Refer to map inset "A" for a diagram of this area. The trail initially parallels Six Mile Run as a grassy doubletrack before turning into singletrack. Check at park office for additional routes and trail updates.

field

seasonal stream

wide grassy path

trail becomes singletrack; follow yellow markings

Six Mile Run

HQ

?

P

Canal Rd.

inset "A"

TRAILS
Y yellow
B blue

SIX MILE RUN RESERVOIR

Y

cross seasonal stream

B blue goes left; follow yellow

Six Mile Run

Y

follow yellow

B rough doubletrack (blue markings)

FRANKLIN TWP.

Y

Intersect blue doubletrack; go right

C Christopher Mac Kinnon 2006

inset "B"

KEEP OUT of field - stay on trail

B

blue trail (rough doubletrack)

B right downhill

old barn

B

B steep uphill

follow signs and singletrack here

see inset "B" for continuation

B

TRAIL RATING: moderate
DISTANCE: apx. 3 miles (round trip)
SURFACE: grass, dirt, rocks, roots, seasonal shallow water crossings

Cheesequake State Park

Cheesequake State Park offers a rare off-road opportunity in an area of the state that is congested and, for the most part, paved over. Although most of the park's trails are off limits to mountain biking, Cheesequake's location and terrain make it a worthwhile destination. Trail usage is light to moderate, which is surprising considering the relatively high population and scarcity of other mountain-biking trails in the immediate area.

In contrast to the gently rolling grassy areas adjacent to the trailhead parking lot, the multi-use trail where mountain biking is permitted is surprisingly technical in spots, with numerous short but steep ascents and descents.

Newly installed white markers make navigation through this area much easier than it used to be. Booth Field Road is the main artery through this section of the park. If you do get disoriented, use it to find your way back to the trailhead. It's a good idea to get a copy of the official park map because it shows Museum Road and many paved roads through the park that are worth exploring.

Park activities are geared toward family recreation and outdoor education. Refer to the multi-colored trail map at the trailhead for the location of the interpretive center off Museum Road. Hooks Creek Lake offers seasonal bathing, with nearby picnic facilities. Reserved campsites are available on a seasonal basis.

A word of caution: The Garden State Parkway commuter lot, which is visible at the end of Booth Field Road, is patrolled by the state police. Don't use it to get to the park, and don't park there.

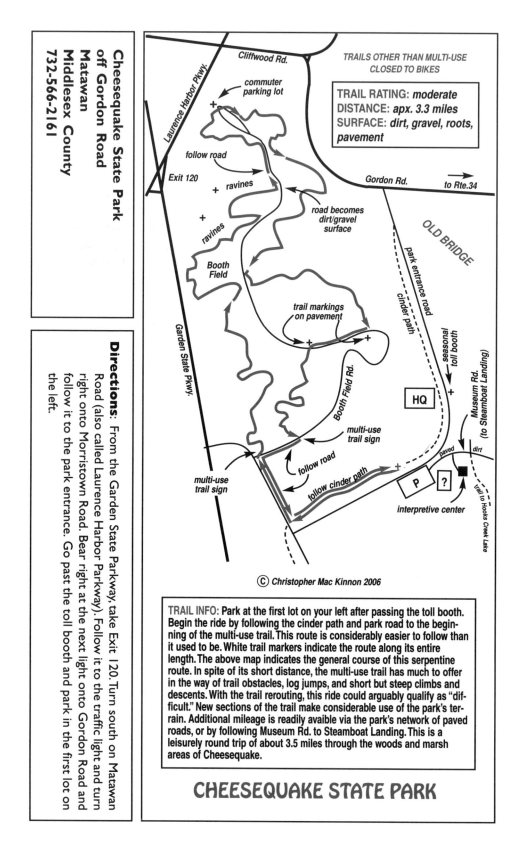

Cheesequake State Park
off of Gordon Road
Matawan
Middlesex County
732-566-2161

TRAILS OTHER THAN MULTI-USE
CLOSED TO BIKES

TRAIL RATING: *moderate*
DISTANCE: *apx. 3.3 miles*
SURFACE: *dirt, gravel, roots, pavement*

Cliffwood Rd.

Laurence Harbor Pkwy.

commuter parking lot

follow road

Exit 120

ravines

ravines

road becomes dirt/gravel surface

Gordon Rd.   to Rte.34

OLD BRIDGE

park entrance road
cinder path

Booth Field

trail markings on pavement

seasonal toll booth

HQ

Garden State Pkwy.

Booth Field Rd.

multi-use trail sign

follow road

multi-use trail sign

follow cinder path

Museum Rd.
(to Steamboat Landing)

paved   dirt

P   ?

trail to Hooks Creek Lake

interpretive center

© *Christopher Mac Kinnon 2006*

Directions: From the Garden State Parkway, take Exit 120. Turn south on Matawan Road (also called Laurence Harbor Parkway). Follow it to the traffic light and turn right onto Morristown Road. Bear right at the next light onto Gordon Road and follow it to the park entrance. Go past the toll booth and park in the first lot on the left.

TRAIL INFO: **Park at the first lot on your left after passing the toll booth. Begin the ride by following the cinder path and park road to the beginning of the multi-use trail. This route is considerably easier to follow than it used to be. White trail markers indicate the route along its entire length. The above map indicates the general course of this serpentine route. In spite of its short distance, the multi-use trail has much to offer in the way of trail obstacles, log jumps, and short but steep climbs and descents. With the trail rerouting, this ride could arguably qualify as "difficult." New sections of the trail make considerable use of the park's terrain. Additional mileage is readily avaible via the park's network of paved roads, or by following Museum Rd. to Steamboat Landing. This is a leisurely round trip of about 3.5 miles through the woods and marsh areas of Cheesequake.**

CHEESEQUAKE STATE PARK

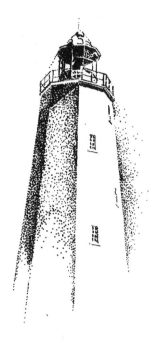

Lighthouse at Sandy Hook

Sandy Hook

Sandy Hook is part of the Gateway National Recreation Area, a sprawling federal park that includes land in three New York City boroughs as well as northern New Jersey. Sandy Hook's 2,044 acres include seven miles of ocean beaches as well as a recently completed multi-use pathway that enables visitors to experience this area by means of two-wheeled transportation.

This ride begins at the Bayberry Beach parking area, just past the park entrance and toll plaza. Cyclists should keep in mind that this is a multi-use trail also open to walkers and in-line skaters. The path extends for several miles, traversing various habitats and environments along the way. The terrain at Sandy Hook ranges from flat to gently inclined.

The southerly portion passes by public beaches and shorebird habitats. Historic highlights include the Nike missile and radar sites as well as the many historic buildings in the Fort Hancock area. Not to be missed is the historic lighthouse, the oldest surviving lighthouse in the U.S. Be sure to stop at the observation deck next to Battery Peck for a spectacular view of the Verrazano Bridge linking Staten Island and Brooklyn.

At 10.8 miles, this is a short but very rewarding ride along one of New Jersey's most famous barrier island environments (though in fact, Sandy Hook is a peninsula). Its proximity to New York City brings unusual traffic in the form of commercial aircraft in the skies above as well as massive ships at sea.

Visible to the south are the distinctive Twin Lights of Navesink, definitely worth a visit. Information about this structure, built in 1862, can be found at **www.twin-lights.org**.

Sandy Hook is perhaps best visited in the off-season, after Labor Day and before Memorial Day. A fee is charged during the summer, and the area tends to be crowded on weekends.

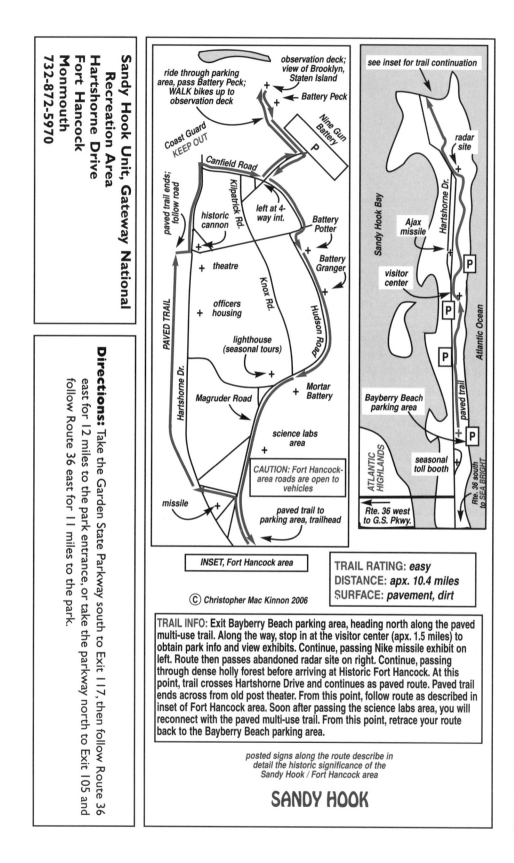

Sandy Hook Unit, Gateway National Recreation Area
Hartshorne Drive
Fort Hancock
Monmouth
732-872-5970

Directions: Take the Garden State Parkway south to Exit 117, then follow Route 36 east for 12 miles to the park entrance, or take the parkway north to Exit 105 and follow Route 36 east for 11 miles to the park.

INSET, Fort Hancock area

© Christopher Mac Kinnon 2006

TRAIL RATING: *easy*
DISTANCE: *apx. 10.4 miles*
SURFACE: *pavement, dirt*

TRAIL INFO: Exit Bayberry Beach parking area, heading north along the paved multi-use trail. Along the way, stop in at the visitor center (apx. 1.5 miles) to obtain park info and view exhibits. Continue, passing Nike missile exhibit on left. Route then passes abandoned radar site on right. Continue, passing through dense holly forest before arriving at Historic Fort Hancock. At this point, trail crosses Hartshorne Drive and continues as paved route. Paved trail ends across from old post theater. From this point, follow route as described in inset of Fort Hancock area. Soon after passing the science labs area, you will reconnect with the paved multi-use trail. From this point, retrace your route back to the Bayberry Beach parking area.

posted signs along the route describe in detail the historic significance of the Sandy Hook / Fort Hancock area

SANDY HOOK

Huber Woods County Park

At about 250 acres, Huber Woods County Park is one of the smallest parcels of land included in this guide. In spite of its relatively small size, however, Huber is a worthwhile off-road destination for a number of reasons, the first being location. It is relatively close to both Hartshorne Woods County Park and the Henry Hudson Trail, and, in addition, it offers the ideal combination of terrain for expert riders to enjoy or for intermediate riders to upgrade their bike-handling skills.

Using the connecting Claypit Run Trail (one of the few soft-sand trails at Huber), many riders combine the trail systems at Huber and Hartshorne Woods. There are enough trails in the two parks to make for a full-day outing. (Refer to the Hartshorne Woods map for the connecting route between these two areas.)

Also, what Huber Woods lacks in size it more than makes up for in trail accessibility. The vast majority of the park's trails are open to bikes, the exception being the nature loop clearly marked at the point where you first enter the woods. Finally, Huber Woods offers a variety of trails, almost all singletrack, ranging from the relatively easy Fox Hollow to the moderately difficult Many Log Run, which probably is the trail most prized by bikers. To these advantages you can add highly visible trail markings, a hard-packed surface, and the allure of the woods itself.

Trails at Huber are primarily multi-use and are color coded according to difficulty. Any attempt to evaluate trail difficulty involves a degree of subjective opinion, but the three categories used here do seem to represent three distinct degrees of difficulty. Look for trail markers at most major intersections. Green circles mark the easiest trails, primarily used by pedestrian traffic, blue squares indicate medium difficulty, and black diamonds are used for the most difficult trails.

Huber Woods trails contain many stretches with blind curves. The park is moderately to heavily used, and cyclists can expect to encounter both equestrian and foot traffic on all the trails.

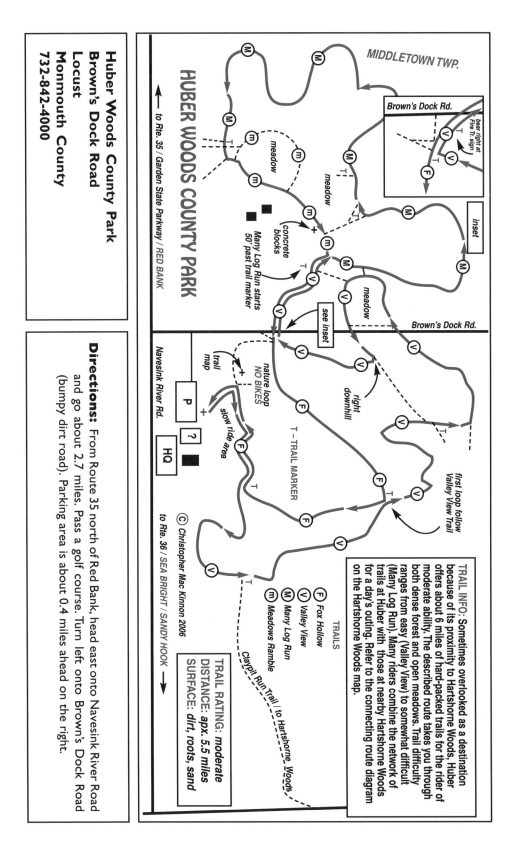

HUBER WOODS COUNTY PARK

MIDDLETOWN TWP.

← to Rte. 35 / Garden State Parkway / RED BANK

Brown's Dock Rd.

bear right at Fire Tr. sign

inset

Brown's Dock Rd.

see inset

meadow

meadow

meadow

meadow

Many Log Run starts 50 past trail marker

concrete blocks

nature loop NO BIKES

right downhill

trail map

slow ride area

first loop follow Valley View Trail

T – TRAIL MARKER

P

?

HQ

Navesink River Rd.

© Christopher Mac Kinnon 2006

to Rte. 36 / SEA BRIGHT / SANDY HOOK →

Claypit Run Trail / to Hartshorne Woods

TRAILS

- (F) Fox Hollow
- (V) Valley View
- (M) Many Log Run
- (m) Meadows Ramble

TRAIL INFO: Sometimes overlooked as a destination because of its proximity to Hartshorne Woods, Huber offers about 6 miles of hard-packed trails for the rider of moderate ability. The described route takes you through both dense forest and open meadows. Trail difficulty ranges from easy (Valley View) to somewhat difficult (Many Log Run). Many riders combine the network of trails at Huber with those at nearby Hartshorne Woods for a day's outing. Refer to the connecting route diagram on the Hartshorne Woods map.

TRAIL RATING: *moderate*
DISTANCE: *apx. 5.5 miles*
SURFACE: *dirt, roots, sand*

Huber Woods County Park
Brown's Dock Road
Locust
Monmouth County
732-842-4000

Directions: From Route 35 north of Red Bank, head east onto Navesink River Road and go about 2.7 miles. Pass a golf course. Turn left onto Brown's Dock Road (bumpy dirt road). Parking area is about 0.4 miles ahead on the right.

Hartshorne Woods County Park

Located near what is arguably the highest point on the eastern seaboard (Mount Mitchell, elevation 266 feet), Hartshorne Woods and the adjacent Twin Lights loom as sentinels overlooking the Atlantic Ocean. It's true, of course, that folks from eastern Maine might laugh at the idea of Mount Mitchell's beating out Maine's 1,530-foot Cadillac Mountain for the title. But the New Jersey peak, located off Route 36 about 1.5 miles east of Hartshorne, rises right along the shoreline, offering wonderful views that reach as far as New York City.

Hartshorne can also boast or weep about its unofficial title as the facility most heavily used by bicyclists in the Monmouth County Park System.

What nearby Huber Woods County Park has on a small scale, Hartshorne has in abundance. Its reputation as a first-class mountain-bike destination is well deserved. A network of well-marked trails takes you through a heavily forested landscape via challenging singletrack. Expect long stretches of hard-packed fast trail, with just enough technical terrain to challenge your bike-handling skills. (Trails in Hartshorne Woods Park are multi-use, so you'll want to stay alert and slow down when approaching blind turns along the trail.)

Mountain-biking opportunities here have been enhanced by the addition of the Rocky Point Trail, a challenging route that explores the hills and valleys of the historic Rocky Point area. If time and energy permit, enjoy a detour that begins where you exit the Rocky Point Trail. A paved multi-use path passes numerous remnants of World War II gun batteries. There's a spectacular view of the Atlantic Ocean from atop the overlook at Battery Lewis. Refer to the posted map as well as trail brochures at the trailhead for further information.

A seasonal view of the Navesink River can be had from the Claypit Creek Overlook. After a steady climb of about a mile, look for a trail marker to the right indicating this overlook. A short trail leads to a vantage point where you can take a breather as well as view the sights along the river.

This ride starts at the Buttermilk Valley Trailhead on Navesink Avenue.

HARTSHORNE WOODS COUNTY PARK

to Rte. 35
RED BANK

Navesink Rd.
to Rte. 36

P

?

DISMOUNT AREA

Kings Hollow,
Candlestick Trails
NO BIKES
ALLOWED

Hartshorne Rd.

Claypit Creek overlook

MIDDLETOWN

cabin

map

dirt road

make loop first

begin Rocky
Point Tr.

Rocky Point
Historical Area

pier

Navesink River

Shrewsbury River

T – TRAIL MARKER

church

cross bridge

Locust Point Rd.
dirt road

Locust Ave.

Claypit Tr.

Hartshorne
trailhead

© Christopher Mac Kinnon 2006

connecting route to Huber Woods apx. 1.25 miles

TRAIL RATING: *difficult*
DISTANCE: *apx. 9.2 miles*
SURFACE: *dirt, sand, rock,
exposed roots, pavement*

TRAIL INFO: This 9.2-mile ride through Hartshorne Woods offers just about everything for the seasoned rider: challenging singletrack with a multitude of obstacles, woods, roads, and rewarding views-- with a little history thrown in. Trails are multi-use and open to bikers, hikers, and equestrians. They are color-coded according to difficulty (red circle=easy, blue square=moderate, black diamond=most diffi-cult). This route consists of moderate and difficult trails. The Laurel Ridge Trail begins as a blue-blazed, eroded uphill at the extreme right of the dismount area. The Cuesta Ridge Trail has one of the longest downhill sections in the state. Refer to the connecting-route diagram on this map to ride to nearby Huber Woods.

TRAILS

- Ⓛ Laurel Ridge
- Ⓖ Grand Tour
- Ⓒ Cuesta Ridge
- Ⓡ Rocky Point

Hartshorne Woods County Park

Navesink Avenue
Middletown
Monmouth County
732-842-4000

Directions: From Route 35 north of Red Bank, turn east onto Navesink River Road. Follow road for about 2.7 miles, passing a golf course. Continue past Brown's Dock Road. Merge with Route 8A, passing Oceanic Bridge on your right. Turn right onto Locust Avenue and cross Claypit Creek. At a large stone church, bear right onto Navesink Avenue. The parking area for Hartshorne Woods is about 0.5 mile ahead on the right.

Henry Hudson trail sign

Henry Hudson Trail

The Henry Hudson Trail is a prime example of the successful reclamation of a resource that had been allowed to fall into a state of disrepair.

The trail was once part of the Jersey Central Railroad, which closed its operations in the area in the mid-1960s. It was seriously neglected before it was finally taken over by the Monmouth County Parks System, which joined residents from the surrounding communities in bringing the abandoned transportation link back to prominence, this time without the once-mighty Iron Horse. Today, you are likely to encounter walkers, joggers, and roller skaters as well as fellow bike riders along the route, which is approximately 10.5 miles long.

The trail surface is paved, and bridges crossing several tidal creeks along the route have been rebuilt, providing views of the surrounding tidal marshes as well as distant glimpses of the lower Manhattan skyline. The trail serves the bayshore towns it runs through (including Keyport, Union Beach, Hazlet, and Keansburg) both as a recreational facility and as a pathway connecting neighborhoods and communities. Flat terrain and the smooth surface make this a good area for young or inexperienced riders.

The trail does continue on past the turn-around point designated on this route map (McMahon Park / Atlantic Avenue), but it comes increasingly closer to the noise and congestion of Route 36 and provides a less pleasant ride. A planned extension of the western end of the trail is expected to bring it through Matawan to Freehold in the next few years, adding another 12 miles to its overall length. Connecting the eastern terminus of the trail with the existing Sandy Hook multi-use trail is also under consideration.

A word of caution: Although the Henry Hudson Trail is open only to non-motorized traffic, it does cross many roads along the way. Cyclists should be aware of traffic at these intersections.

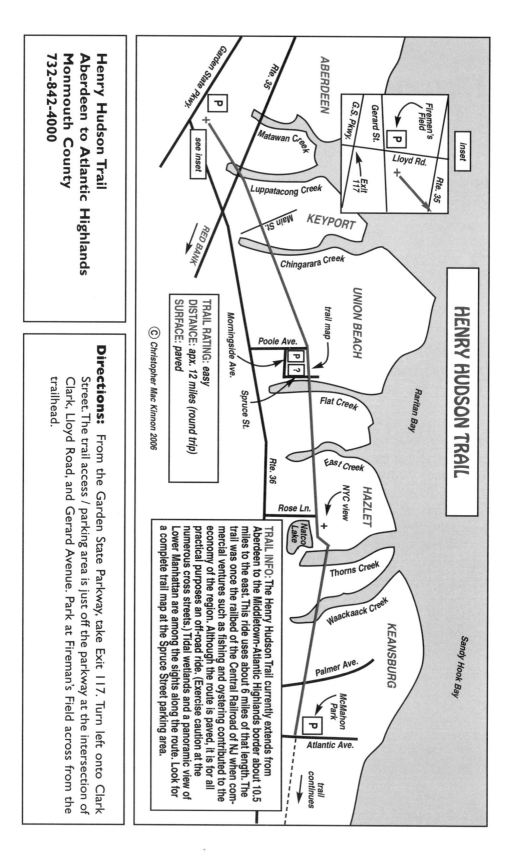

HENRY HUDSON TRAIL

**Henry Hudson Trail
Aberdeen to Atlantic Highlands
Monmouth County
732-842-4000**

Directions: From the Garden State Parkway, take Exit 117. Turn left onto Clark Street. The trail access / parking area is just off the parkway at the intersection of Clark, Lloyd Road, and Gerard Avenue. Park at Fireman's Field across from the trailhead.

© Christopher Mac Kinnon 2006

TRAIL RATING: **easy**
DISTANCE: **apx. 12 miles (round trip)**
SURFACE: **paved**

TRAIL INFO: The Henry Hudson Trail currently extends from Aberdeen to the Middletown-Atlantic Highlands border about 10.5 miles to the east. This ride uses about 6 miles of that length. The trail was once the railbed of the Central Railroad of NJ when commercial ventures such as fishing and oystering contributed to the economy of the region. Although the route is paved, it is for all practical purposes an off-road ride. (Exercise caution at the numerous cross streets.) Tidal wetlands and a panoramic view of Lower Manhattan are among the sights along the route. Look for a complete trail map at the Spruce Street parking area.

ABERDEEN

KEYPORT

UNION BEACH

HAZLET

KEANSBURG

Raritan Bay

Sandy Hook Bay

Garden State Pkwy.

Rte. 35

Matawan Creek

Luppatacong Creek

Chingarara Creek

Main St.

RED BANK

Morningside Ave.

Poole Ave.

Spruce St.

Flat Creek

East Creek

Rose Ln.

Natco Lake

NYC view

Thorns Creek

Waackaack Creek

Palmer Ave.

McMahon Park

Atlantic Ave.

trail continues

Rte. 36

trail map

see inset

inset

Fireman's Field

G.S. Pkwy.

Gerard St.

Lloyd Rd.

Exit 117

Rte. 35

Thompson County Park

Thompson County Park's 665 acres provide diverse recreational opportunities. This former horse farm has both the expected and the unexpected in a county park. Its many athletic fields host soccer, lacrosse, and rugby teams and tournaments. Pottery classes and live theater are also held here. Anglers can fish in Lake Marlu either by boat or from the shore.

A paved multi-use trail about 1.8 miles in length bisects the park and is part of this 6.3-mile route. The ride gives an overview of the park landscape. It begins and ends at the parking area near the visitor center. This splendid structure, which also served as the headquarters of the Monmouth County Park System, suffered a devastating fire in February 2006.

The described route winds its way through open fields populated with sizable trees. A highlight along the way is the one-mile horse-training oval. The park, formerly an estate called Brookdale Farm, was a first-rate breeding and training facility for racehorses. With a little imagination one can easily conjure up images of thoroughbreds going through their paces here.

Continue your ride via grassy dirt roads, passing by buildings once used in conjunction with the horse facility as well as the Swimming River Reservoir. Thompson provides an enjoyable and interesting ride for cyclists of all levels of ability.

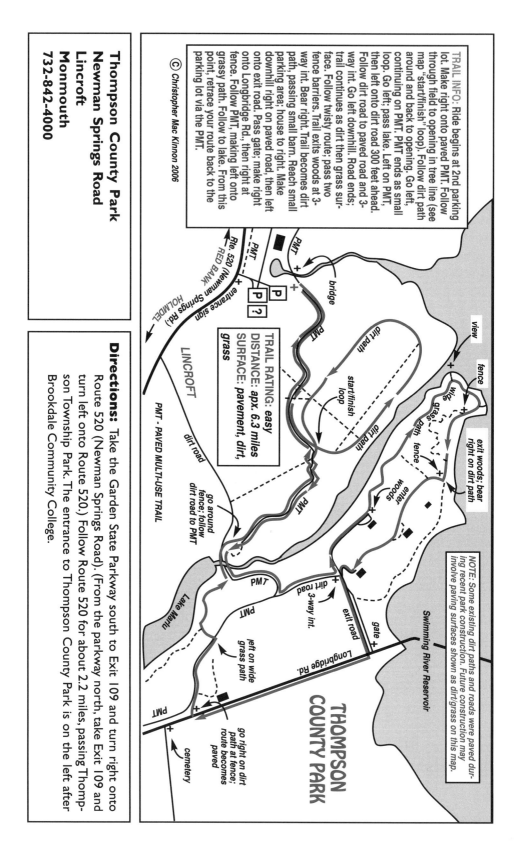

TRAIL INFO: Ride begins at 2nd parking lot. Make right onto paved PMT. Follow through field to opening in tree line (see map "start/finish" loop). Follow dirt path around and back to opening. Go left, continuing on PMT. PMT ends as small loop. Go left; pass lake. Left on PMT, then left onto dirt road 300 feet ahead. Follow dirt road to paved road and 3-way int. Go left downhill. Road ends; trail continues as dirt then grass surface. Follow twisty route; pass two fence barriers. Trail exits woods at 3-way int. Bear right. Trail becomes dirt path, passing small barn. Reach small parking area; house to right. Make downhill right on paved road, then left onto exit road. Pass gate; make right onto Longbridge Rd., then right at fence. Follow PMT, making left onto grassy path. Follow to lake. From this point, retrace your route back to the parking lot via the PMT.

© Christopher Mac Kinnon 2006

NOTE: Some existing dirt paths and roads were paved during recent park construction. Future construction may involve paving surfaces shown as dirt/grass on this map.

TRAIL RATING: easy
DISTANCE: apx. 6.3 miles
SURFACE: pavement, dirt, grass

PMT - PAVED MULTI-USE TRAIL

THOMPSON COUNTY PARK

Swimming River Reservoir

LINCROFT

Rte. 520 (Newman Springs Rd.)
RED BANK
HOLMDEL

Lake Marlu

Longbridge Rd.

start/finish loop

dirt path

bridge

view

fence

exit woods; bear right on dirt path

enter woods

go around fence; follow dirt road to PMT

dirt road

3-way int.

exit road

gate

cemetery

go right on dirt path at fence; route becomes paved

left on wide grass path

wide grass path fence

entrance sign

P P ?

PMT

Thompson County Park
Newman Springs Road
Lincroft
Monmouth
732-842-4000

Directions: Take the Garden State Parkway south to Exit 109 and turn right onto Route 520 (Newman Springs Road). (From the parkway north, take Exit 109 and turn left onto Route 520.) Follow Route 520 for about 2.2 miles, passing Thompson Township Park. The entrance to Thompson County Park is on the left after Brookdale Community College.

Tatum County Park

This 3.8-mile ride through Tatum County Park may be relatively short, but its combination of open fields and secluded singletrack make a pleasant outing for the intermediate rider.

The route uses two of the park's multi-use trails, Tatum Ramble and Meadow Run. Both are indicated by blue square markings. The park's rolling terrain of woodland and fields is accessible by a number of trails and dirt roads, but riders should note that the Holly Grove Trail, the Dogwood Trail, and portions of the Indian Springs Trail are all closed to bicycle traffic.

The property that is Tatum Park today was purchased in 1905 by Charles Tatum of New York City, a manufacturer of commercial glassware. The fields that are part of the described route were first cleared and cultivated around 1920. A donation of 75 acres in 1975 by a member of the Tatum family marked the beginning of what is now Tatum Park, which is part of the Monmouth County Park System.

Subsequent purchases over the years increased the park to its present size of 368 acres. The Holland Activity Center, located next to the parking lot, is home to the Monmouth Conservation Foundation, a group instrumental in land acquisition for preservation in Monmouth County.

A 5-minute drive to the Red Hill Activity Center located off Red Hill Road is a good way to extend your day's outing to Tatum Park. Here you will find the Holly Grove Trail, a short, half-mile loop through a magnificent grove of holly trees (foot traffic only). Across from the Red Hill Activity Center parking area is the entrance to Deep Cut Gardens, a county-owned horticultural masterpiece, dedicated to the home gardener.

To reach this area, turn right onto Van Schoick Road after exiting the park. At the first intersection, turn right onto Holland Road. (Don't try to bike to this area, because Red Hill Road is narrow, with many blind curves.)

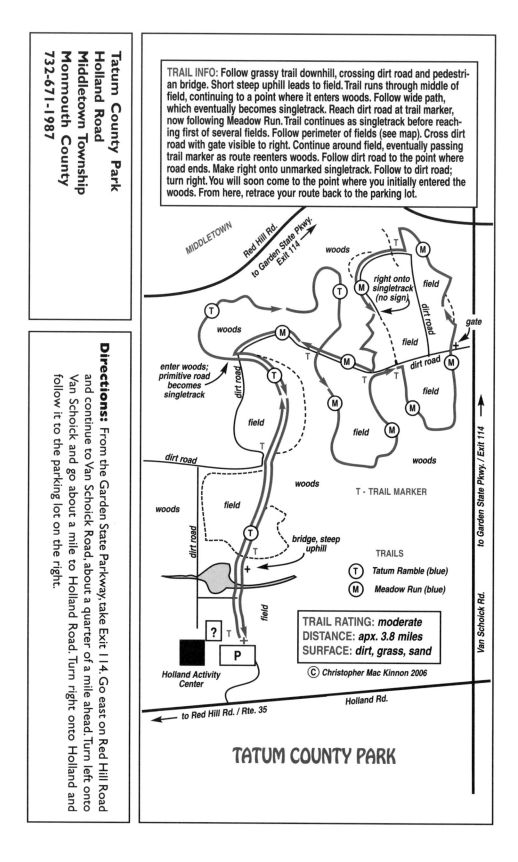

Tatum County Park
Holland Road
Middletown Township
Monmouth County
732-671-1987

TRAIL INFO: Follow grassy trail downhill, crossing dirt road and pedestrian bridge. Short steep uphill leads to field. Trail runs through middle of field, continuing to a point where it enters woods. Follow wide path, which eventually becomes singletrack. Reach dirt road at trail marker, now following Meadow Run. Trail continues as singletrack before reaching first of several fields. Follow perimeter of fields (see map). Cross dirt road with gate visible to right. Continue around field, eventually passing trail marker as route reenters woods. Follow dirt road to the point where road ends. Make right onto unmarked singletrack. Follow to dirt road; turn right. You will soon come to the point where you initially entered the woods. From here, retrace your route back to the parking lot.

Directions: From the Garden State Parkway, take Exit 114. Go east on Red Hill Road and continue to Van Schoick Road, about a quarter of a mile ahead. Turn left onto Van Schoick and go about a mile to Holland Road. Turn right onto Holland and follow it to the parking lot on the right.

MIDDLETOWN

Red Hill Rd.

to Garden State Pkwy. Exit 114

woods

right onto singletrack (no sign)

field

dirt road

gate

woods

enter woods; primitive road becomes singletrack

dirt road

field

field

dirt road

field

woods

dirt road

woods

field

woods

T - TRAIL MARKER

to Garden State Pkwy. / Exit 114

Van Scholck Rd.

dirt road

woods

field

bridge, steep uphill

TRAILS

(T) Tatum Ramble (blue)

(M) Meadow Run (blue)

field

? T

P

Holland Activity Center

TRAIL RATING: *moderate*
DISTANCE: *apx. 3.8 miles*
SURFACE: *dirt, grass, sand*

© Christopher Mac Kinnon 2006

to Red Hill Rd. / Rte. 35

Holland Rd.

TATUM COUNTY PARK

Joe Palaia Township Park

A casual rider friend introduced me to Joe Palaia Township Park. Unable to persuade him to venture to either Allaire or Cheesequake, I agreed to meet him here. Several laps around the well-designed 3-mile circuit trail provided a nice change of pace from the serious workouts at other locations nearby.

The park has an interesting history. The property was first developed as a farm, and a well-preserved mastodon skeleton, since lost, was discovered there in the early 19th century. Later known as the Deal Test Site, it was used for communications purposes by AT&T, and three tall towers used to communicate with ships still stand. Later still, it was used by the Army in tracking satellites. It was purchased by Ocean Township in the early 1970s and was subsequently developed as a park.

Half of the park is open space and the other half is covered with vegetation including a swamp forest, wetlands, and an area of seashore vegetation. The area is popular with birders in May and September. There is an osprey nest on one of the towers, and ospreys have been seen hunting for fish nearby.

Recent expansion has added 42 acres to the park, bringing it to a total of 250 acres, and Ocean Township is working on a plan to extend the trail system into the new area.

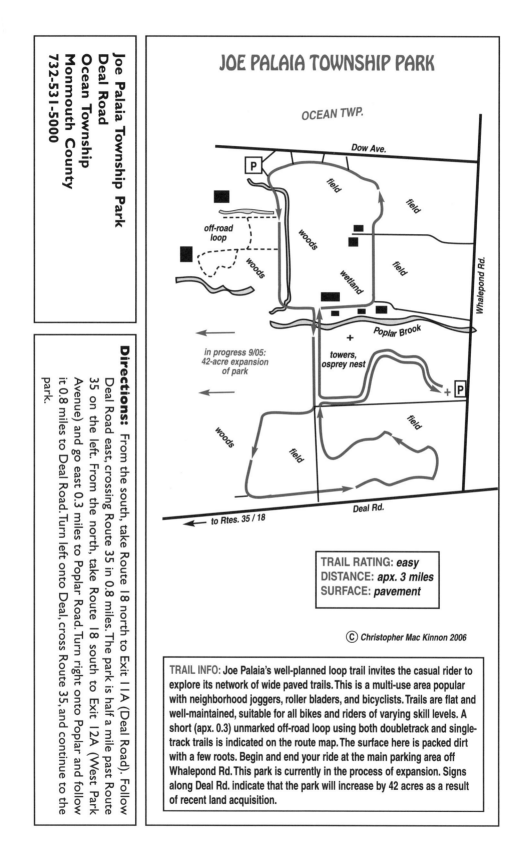

JOE PALAIA TOWNSHIP PARK

OCEAN TWP.

Dow Ave.

P

field

field

off-road loop

woods

woods

field

wetland

Whalepond Rd.

Poplar Brook

in progress 9/05: 42-acre expansion of park

towers, osprey nest

P

woods

field

field

field

Deal Rd.

← to Rtes. 35 / 18

Joe Palaia Township Park
Deal Road
Ocean Township
Monmouth County
732-531-5000

Directions: From the south, take Route 18 north to Exit 11A (Deal Road). Follow Deal Road east, crossing Route 35 in 0.8 miles. The park is half a mile past Route 35 on the left. From the north, take Route 18 south to Exit 12A (West Park Avenue) and go east 0.3 miles to Poplar Road. Turn right onto Poplar and follow it 0.8 miles to Deal Road. Turn left onto Deal, cross Route 35, and continue to the park.

TRAIL RATING: *easy*
DISTANCE: *apx. 3 miles*
SURFACE: *pavement*

© *Christopher Mac Kinnon 2006*

TRAIL INFO: Joe Palaia's well-planned loop trail invites the casual rider to explore its network of wide paved trails. This is a multi-use area popular with neighborhood joggers, roller bladers, and bicyclists. Trails are flat and well-maintained, suitable for all bikes and riders of varying skill levels. A short (apx. 0.3) unmarked off-road loop using both doubletrack and single-track trails is indicated on the route map. The surface here is packed dirt with a few roots. Begin and end your ride at the main parking area off Whalepond Rd. This park is currently in the process of expansion. Signs along Deal Rd. indicate that the park will increase by 42 acres as a result of recent land acquisition.

Shark River County Park

Located on the border of Wall and Neptune Townships in southern Monmouth County, Shark River Park is easily accessible from the Garden State Parkway or Routes 34 and 18. At 588 acres, it is one of the mid-size parks within the Monmouth County Park System. In addition to cycling, Shark River offers opportunities for fishing and hiking, and it includes a playground and a fitness trail.

Though not as well known as other Monmouth County destinations such as Hartshorne or Huber Woods, this park offers trails that are best suited for novice to moderately skilled riders. It is the perfect destination for the cyclist wanting to venture onto singletrack trail without having to deal with a multitude of trail obstacles.

Most of this route uses the park's network of hard-packed, wide, flat to rolling woods paths. For lack of a better description, they are referred to as "trails," both on the posted map at the trailhead and on our route map of the area.

Despite its proximity to both the Garden State Parkway and the surrounding neighborhoods, this ride includes areas where you will experience the feeling of being in a remote wooded area.

The Hidden Creek Trail is marked as multi-use. Stay alert on the singletrack portions of this trail. There are several short trails on the other side of Schoolhouse Road. This is the primary day-use area of the park and as a result it is sometimes quite congested, so it is best avoided by cyclists.

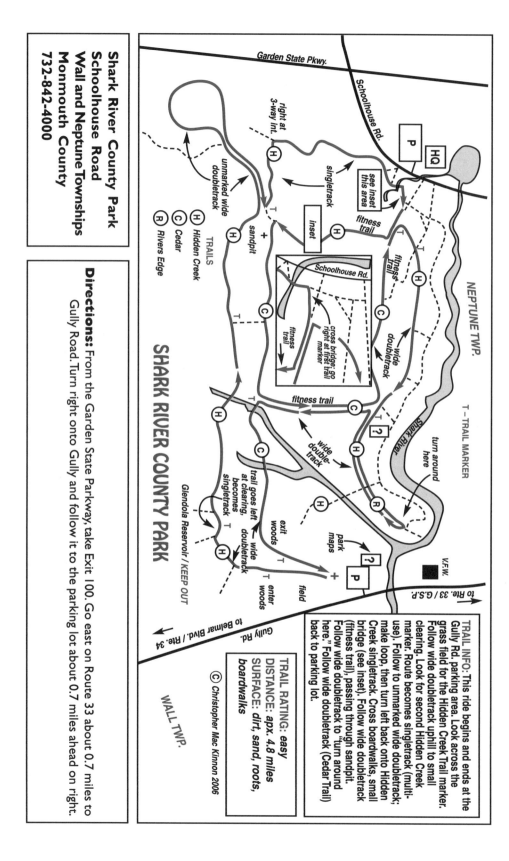

Shark River County Park
Schoolhouse Road
Wall and Neptune Townships
Monmouth County
732-842-4000

Directions: From the Garden State Parkway, take Exit 100. Go east on Route 33 about 0.7 miles to Gully Road. Turn right onto Gully and follow it to the parking lot about 0.7 miles ahead on right.

SHARK RIVER COUNTY PARK

NEPTUNE TWP.

T – TRAIL MARKER

to Rte. 33 / G.S.P.

V.F.W.

Garden State Pkwy.

Schoolhouse Rd.

P

HQ

see inset this area

inset

fitness trail

singletrack

right at 3-way int.

unmarked wide doubletrack

sandpit

TRAILS
(H) Hidden Creek
(C) Cedar
(R) Rivers Edge

Schoolhouse Rd.

cross bridge; go right at first trail marker

fitness trail

wide doubletrack

turn around here

Shark River

?

fitness trail

wide double-track

trail goes left at clearing, becomes singletrack

wide doubletrack

exit woods

enter woods

field

park maps

?

P

Glendola Reservoir / KEEP OUT

to Belmar Blvd. / Rte. 34

Gully Rd.

WALL TWP.

© Christopher Mac Kinnon 2006

TRAIL INFO: This ride begins and ends at the Gully Rd. parking area. Look across the grass field for the Hidden Creek Trail marker. Follow wide doubletrack uphill to small clearing. Look for second Hidden Creek marker. Route becomes singletrack (multi-use). Follow to unmarked wide doubletrack; make loop, then turn left back onto Hidden Creek singletrack. Cross boardwalks, small bridge (see inset). Follow wide doubletrack (fitness trail), passing through sandpit. Follow wide doubletrack to "turn around here." Follow wide doubletrack (Cedar Trail) back to parking lot.

TRAIL RATING: easy
DISTANCE: apx. 4.8 miles
SURFACE: dirt, sand, roots, boardwalks

Allaire State Park

The restored 1830s village at Allaire State Park is a first-rate example of historical restoration. This old iron-making village has an outstanding collection of buildings and artifacts from the era, with guides in period costumes. It is definitely worth a look before or after your ride, but it is strictly for pedestrians—no bikes allowed.

A good portion of the park lies south of both the village area and the Manasquan River. This is where bicyclists are allowed on the multi-use trails, which are also frequented by hikers and equestrians. To get here from the village, go east on Route 524 for about 2 miles. Turn right onto Hospital Road. About a mile ahead there is a large dirt parking area on the right. Signs here provide trail updates and precautionary information regarding hunting and a persistent seasonal tick problem.

The updated trail-information map, provided courtesy of ATUG (Allaire Trail User Group), reflects renovations and designations at Allaire. The orange trail is about 4.6 miles long, the blue trail is 3.1 miles, and the white trail is 2.3 miles. Each offers a sample of what the area is like as a whole, including singletrack and wide fire roads and areas of "sugar sand" as well as hard-packed surface.

The orange trail continues past the point indicated on the route map and in fact is the outermost loop of the three. Unfortunately, it has some sections that are virtually unridable due to heavy concentration of sugar sand.

As you ride, you will notice many trail markings not indicated on the accompanying map. They are unreliable and perhaps outdated. Until you get to know the area, it is probably best to stick to the described route.

Since the area does have a reputation for ticks, we recommend that warm-weather riders make an effort to stay on the wider trails if possible, avoid areas that are wet or have tall grass, and wear light-colored clothing to make it easier to spot any ticks that have found you. We prefer to ride here in colder weather for two reasons: to avoid ticks, and also because there is a better chance that at least some of the sugar sand found here will have become hard-packed. See page 18 for more information on ticks.

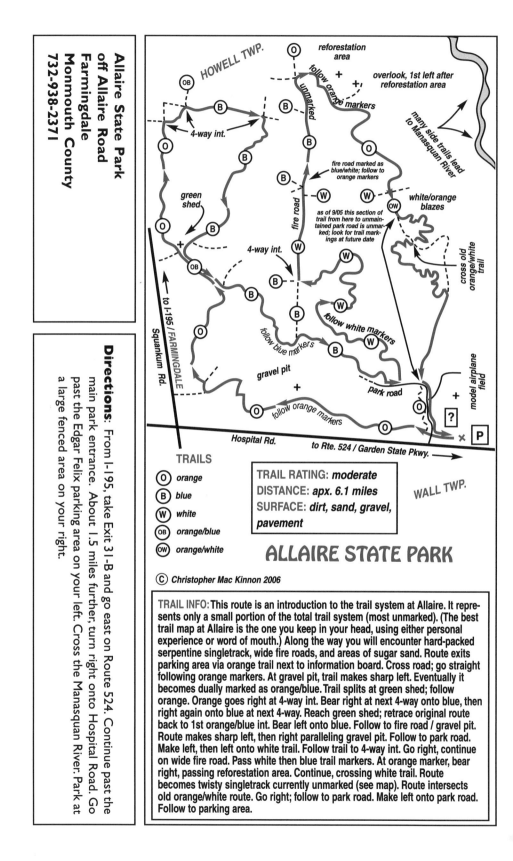

Allaire State Park
off Allaire Road
Farmingdale
Monmouth County
732-938-2371

Directions: From I-195, take Exit 31-B and go east on Route 524. Continue past the main park entrance. About 1.5 miles further, turn right onto Hospital Road. Go past the Edgar Felix parking area on your left. Cross the Manasquan River. Park at a large fenced area on your right.

HOWELL TWP.

reforestation area

overlook, 1st left after reforestation area

follow orange markers

unmarked

many side trails lead to Manasquan River

4-way int.

fire road marked as blue/white; follow to orange markers

green shed

white/orange blazes

as of 9/05 this section of trail from here to unmaintained park road is unmarked; look for trail markings at future date

cross old orange/white trail

4-way int.

to I-195 / FARMINGDALE

Squankum Rd.

4-way int.

follow white markers

follow blue markers

gravel pit

model airplane field

follow orange markers

park road

Hospital Rd.

to Rte. 524 / Garden State Pkwy.

P

?

WALL TWP.

TRAILS

- (O) orange
- (B) blue
- (W) white
- (OB) orange/blue
- (OW) orange/white

TRAIL RATING: *moderate*
DISTANCE: *apx. 6.1 miles*
SURFACE: *dirt, sand, gravel, pavement*

ALLAIRE STATE PARK

© *Christopher Mac Kinnon 2006*

TRAIL INFO: This route is an introduction to the trail system at Allaire. It represents only a small portion of the total trail system (most unmarked). (The best trail map at Allaire is the one you keep in your head, using either personal experience or word of mouth.) Along the way you will encounter hard-packed serpentine singletrack, wide fire roads, and areas of sugar sand. Route exits parking area via orange trail next to information board. Cross road; go straight following orange markers. At gravel pit, trail makes sharp left. Eventually it becomes dually marked as orange/blue. Trail splits at green shed; follow orange. Orange goes right at 4-way int. Bear right at next 4-way onto blue, then right again onto blue at next 4-way. Reach green shed; retrace original route back to 1st orange/blue int. Bear left onto blue. Follow to fire road / gravel pit. Route makes sharp left, then right paralleling gravel pit. Follow to park road. Make left, then left onto white trail. Follow trail to 4-way int. Go right, continue on wide fire road. Pass white then blue trail markers. At orange marker, bear right, passing reforestation area. Continue, crossing white trail. Route becomes twisty singletrack currently unmarked (see map). Route intersects old orange/white route. Go right; follow to park road. Make left onto park road. Follow to parking area.

Sign at Allaire State Park

Allenwood General Store

Edgar Felix Bikeway

The Edgar Felix Bikeway runs from Allaire State Park to the seaside community of Manasquan in eastern Monmouth County. The route follows an abandoned railroad right-of-way, now paved. The smooth surface allows for use by all types of bicycles.

This is a moderately to heavily trafficked multi-use trail, and you can expect to encounter just about anything with two or more wheels along the way. It's a good idea to ride slowly. In many places, the path runs right next to private property, and local residents in the area seem to regard it as an extension of their own backyards.

The ride begins at the large parking area beside Atlantic Avenue (Route 524) near 18th Avenue. Orchard Park, near the end of the route, contains tennis courts and a basketball court, as well as swings and a play area for children. Once you reach Manasquan, you can get to the beach area by turning right onto Main Street and following it downtown, crossing Route 71, and continuing to the beach.

Another approach to this ride is to park at the municipal lot on North Main Street in Manasquan and follow the route in reverse. Mountain bikers from the Manasquan-Brielle area use the Edgar Felix Bikeway as a connecting route to and from nearby Allaire State Park.

The restored 1830s period village at Allaire is worth exploring. The vintage Pine Creek Railroad, shown in the map inset, operates on a seasonal basis. Inquire at the ticket booth next to the main parking area for schedules and fees.

The newly completed Wall Township Bikeway (see map) connects the Edgar Felix Trail to the Wall Township Municipal Complex on Allaire Road.

EDGAR FELIX BIKEWAY

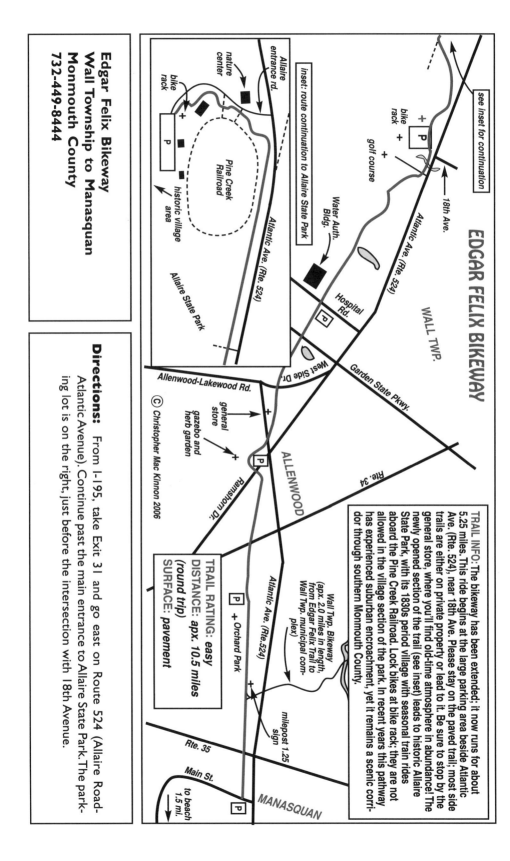

see inset for continuation

WALL TWP.

bike rack

Atlantic Ave. (Rte. 524)

18th Ave.

golf course

Water Auth. Bldg.

Hospital Rd.

Allaire entrance rd.

nature center

bike rack

Pine Creek Railroad

historic village area

Atlantic Ave. (Rte. 524)

Allaire State Park

inset: route continuation to Allaire State Park

© Christopher Mac Kinnon 2006

Allenwood-Lakewood Rd.

West Side Dr.

Garden State Pkwy.

general store

gazebo and herb garden

Ramshorn Dr.

ALLENWOOD

Rte. 34

Atlantic Ave. (Rte. 524)

Orchard Park

milepost 1.25 sign

Wall Twp. Bikeway (apx. 2.0 miles in length, from Edgar Felix Trail to Wall Twp. municipal complex)

Rte. 35

Main St.

to beach 1.5 mi.

MANASQUAN

TRAIL INFO: The bikeway has been extended; it now runs for about 5.25 miles. This ride begins at the large parking area beside Atlantic Ave. (Rte. 524), near 18th Ave. Please stay on the paved trail; most side trails are either on private property or lead to it. Be sure to stop by the general store, where you'll find old-time atmosphere in abundance! The newly opened section of the trail (see inset) leads to historic Allaire State Park, with its 1830s period village with seasonal train rides aboard the Pine Creek Railroad. Lock bikes at bike rack; they are not allowed in the village section of the park. In recent years this pathway has experienced suburban encroachment, yet it remains a scenic corridor through southern Monmouth County.

TRAIL RATING: easy
DISTANCE: apx. 10.5 miles (round trip)
SURFACE: pavement

Edgar Felix Bikeway
Wall Township to Manasquan
Monmouth County
732-449-8444

Directions: From I-195, take Exit 31 and go east on Route 524 (Allaire Road-Atlantic Avenue). Continue past the main entrance to Allaire State Park. The parking lot is on the right, just before the intersection with 18th Avenue.

Manasquan Reservoir

In addition to providing a supply of drinking water, Manasquan Reservoir serves as a wildlife habitat and recreation area for southern Monmouth County.

This ride follows the perimeter trail, which is approximately 5 miles long and mostly level, with a few gradual inclines. The ride begins and ends at the main park entrance road. From the parking lot, backtrack towards the tollbooth. The trail crosses the entrance road at a diagonal 25 feet before the toll. Look for a small sign indicating the trail entrance, and bear right, following the trail.

A number of unmarked side trails intersect the obvious wide main cinder/dirt trail. If you travel in a clockwise direction as indicated by the directional arrows on the map, trails to the right of the main route head in the direction of the reservoir; trails to the left lead either to private property or to one of the surrounding perimeter roads.

The reservoir, which is adjacent to the Howell Park Golf Course, is a great place for a family outing, with a number of other activities besides bicycling available to round out the day.

Bird watching is a popular activity in the park, and the Chestnut Point parking area is a well-known fishing spot. From this area, an eerie forest of dead trees rises from the waters of the reservoir. Non-motorized boats can be launched for a small fee, and rowboats and kayaks can be rented. Guided boat tours are also available. Check at the park office for details.

Caution: Weekend use at Manasquan Reservoir ranges from moderate to heavy. The perimeter trail is multi-use and traveled in both directions. Along the route there are numerous blind corners. Ride with care!

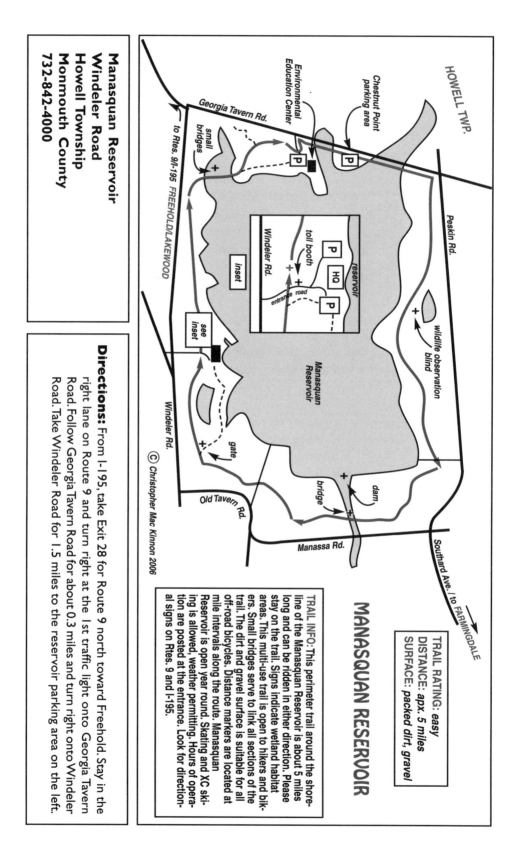

MANASQUAN RESERVOIR

TRAIL RATING: *easy*
DISTANCE: *apx. 5 miles*
SURFACE: *packed dirt, gravel*

TRAIL INFO: This perimeter trail around the shore-line of the Manasquan Reservoir is about 5 miles long and can be ridden in either direction. Please stay on the trail. Signs indicate wetland habitat areas. This multi-use trail is open to hikers and bikers. Small bridges serve to link all sections of the trail. The dirt and gravel surface is suitable for all off-road bicycles. Distance markers are located at mile intervals along the route. Manasquan Reservoir is open year round. Skating and XC ski-ing is allowed, weather permitting. Hours of operation are posted at the entrance. Look for direction-al signs on Rtes. 9 and I-195.

Directions: From I-195, take Exit 28 for Route 9 north toward Freehold. Stay in the right lane on Route 9 and turn right at the 1st traffic light onto Georgia Tavern Road. Follow Georgia Tavern Road for about 0.3 miles and turn right onto Windeler Road. Take Windeler Road for 1.5 miles to the reservoir parking area on the left.

Manasquan Reservoir
Windeler Road
Howell Township
Monmouth County
732-842-4000

© Christopher Mac Kinnon 2006

Assunpink Wildlife Management Area

The Assunpink Wildlife Management area is located in extreme western Monmouth County, in the approximate geographic center of the state.

Despite its proximity to encroaching development, it is still a haven for wildlife native to the area, as well as a stopover for migrating birds. Assunpink's 5,700 acres offer many attractions to the human population as well. The name Assunpink is said to have originated from a Lenape Indian word that can be translated "rocky place that is watery." A network of artificial lakes resulting from the damming of Assunpink Creek provides excellent fishing opportunities. Chain pickerel and crappies are among the many species to be found here. Seasonal hunting and field trials are also popular at Assunpink. (See page 21 for more information on the WMA system, including the New Jersey Fish and Wildlife Division's official policies on riding in these areas.)

Although some of the terrain in this area is similar to what you'd find several miles south at Clayton County Park, the route was designed with the casual rider in mind. It uses the area's network of unpaved and paved roads. Both are open to vehicular traffic. County Route 524 is a light- to moderately-used country road, popular with area bike clubs.

A short section of the route follows one of the many wooded paths to be found in the area. It is indicated on the map east of the former regional Wildlife Management Area office. If heavy rain or summer overgrowth makes the trail difficult to ride, you can bypass it by continuing past the gate until you reach the WMA office, then turning left onto the paved road also shown on the map.

Note: This area is also popular with equestrians and has many trails intended for horses. These equestrian trails can be easily identified by manmade obstacles, low fences, log piles, stone walls, and so forth. In the interest of both courtesy and safety, cyclists are encouraged to avoid the equestrian trails.

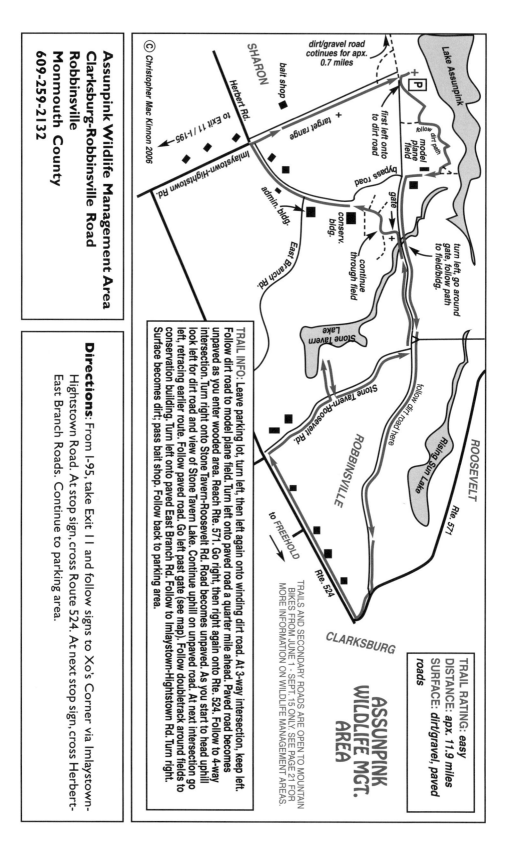

Assunpink Wildlife Management Area
Clarksburg-Robbinsville Road
Robbinsville
Monmouth County
609-259-2132

ⓒ Christopher Mac Kinnon 2006

Directions: From I-95, take Exit 11 and follow signs to Xo's Corner via Imlaystown-Hightstown Road. At stop sign, cross Route 524. At next stop sign, cross Herbert-East Branch Roads. Continue to parking area.

TRAIL RATING: *easy*
DISTANCE: *apx. 11.9 miles*
SURFACE: *dirt/gravel, paved roads*

ASSUNPINK WILDLIFE MGT. AREA

TRAILS AND SECONDARY ROADS ARE OPEN TO MOUNTAIN BIKES FROM JUNE 1 - SEPT. 15 ONLY. SEE PAGE 21 FOR MORE INFORMATION ON WILDLIFE MANAGEMENT AREAS.

TRAIL INFO: Leave parking lot, turn left, then left again onto winding dirt road. At 3-way intersection, keep left. Follow dirt road to model plane field. Turn left onto paved road a quarter mile ahead. Paved road becomes unpaved as you enter wooded area. Reach Rte. 571. Go right, then right again onto Rte. 524. Follow to 4-way intersection. Turn right onto Stone Tavern-Roosevelt Rd. Road becomes unpaved. As you start to head uphill look left for dirt road and view of Stone Tavern Lake. Continue uphill on unpaved road. At next intersection go left, retracing earlier route. Follow paved road. Go left past gate (see map). Follow doubletrack around fields to conservation building. Turn left onto paved East Branch Rd. Follow to Imlaystown-Hightstown Rd. Turn right. Surface becomes dirt; pass bait shop. Follow back to parking area.

Map labels: Lake Assunpink · P · SHARON · Herbert Rd. · Imlaystown-Hightstown Rd. · to Exit 11 / I-195 · bait shop · target range · model plane field · dirt/gravel road cotinues for apx. 0.7 miles · follow dirt path · first left onto to dirt road · bypass road · gate · turn left, go around gate, follow path to field/bldg. · continue through field · admin. bldg. · conserv. bldg. · East Branch Rd. · Stone Tavern Lake · Stone Tavern-Roosevelt Rd. · ROBBINSVILLE · follow dirt road here · Rising Sun Lake · ROOSEVELT · Rte. 571 · to FREEHOLD · Rte. 524 · CLARKSBURG

Clayton County Park

Clayton County Park is proof that good things do indeed sometimes come in small packages. Although relatively small in size at 390 acres, the park is well suited for intermediate riders as well as less-experienced riders looking to upgrade their skills.

Clayton Woods is one of the least developed sites in the Monmouth County Park System. Located in Upper Freehold Township, the westernmost, less-populated part of Monmouth County, it is also one of the most isolated.

Clayton is about halfway between Mercer County Park to the west and Allaire State Park to the east, and it features the best aspects of both areas. Here you can find the hilly terrain of Allaire minus the sand, as well as the hard-packed singletrack characteristic of Mercer.

You can extend your day's outing by exploring the lightly trafficked country roads in the area. Old barns and horse farms dot the landscape in this part of Monmouth County, and despite recent development in the area, it still retains a rural atmosphere.

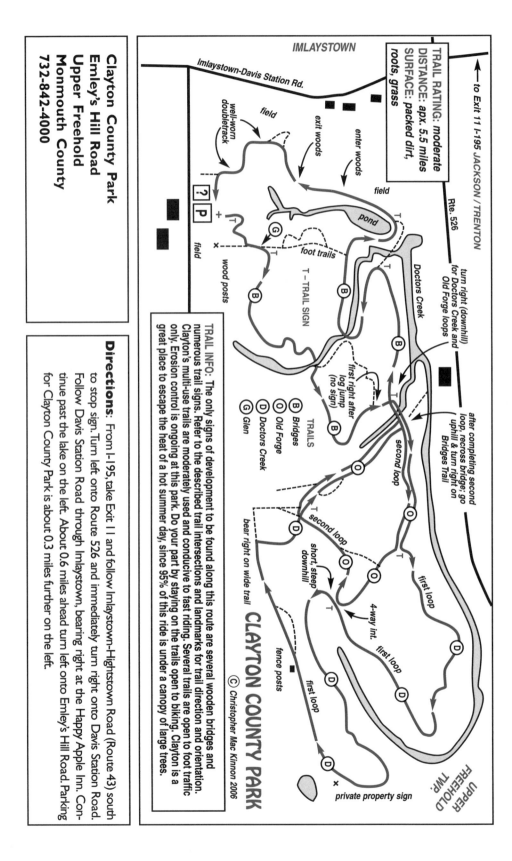

CLAYTON COUNTY PARK

© Christopher Mac Kinnon 2006

TRAIL RATING: *moderate*
DISTANCE: *apx. 5.5 miles*
SURFACE: *packed dirt, roots, grass*

IMLAYSTOWN

Imlaystown-Davis Station Rd.

to Exit 11 I-195 JACKSON / TRENTON

Rte. 526

well-worn doubletrack

field

exit woods

enter woods

field

pond

turn right (downhill) for Doctors Creek and Old Forge loops

Doctors Creek

after completing second loop, recross bridge; go uphill & turn right on Bridges Trail

?

P

+

field

wood posts

T - TRAIL SIGN

G

B

B

foot trails

B

first right after log jump (no sign)

B

second loop

O

second loop

O

D

bear right on wide trail

O

T

O

first loop

short, steep downhill

T

4-way int.

first loop

D

fence posts

D

first loop

D

private property sign

UPPER FREEHOLD TWP.

TRAILS

- **B** Bridges
- **O** Old Forge
- **D** Doctors Creek
- **G** Glen

TRAIL INFO: The only signs of development to be found along this route are several wooden bridges and numerous trail signs. Refer to the described trail intersections and landmarks for trail direction and orientation. Clayton's multi-use trails are moderately used and conducive to fast riding. Several trails are open to biking. Clayton is a great place to escape the heat of a hot summer day, since 95% of this ride is under a canopy of large trees. Erosion control is ongoing at this park. Do your part by staying on the trails open to foot traffic only.

Directions: From I-195, take Exit 11 and follow Imlaystown-Hightstown Road (Route 43) south to stop sign. Turn left onto Route 526 and immediately turn right onto Davis Station Road. Follow Davis Station Road through Imlaystown, bearing right at the Happy Apple Inn. Continue past the lake on the left. About 0.6 miles ahead turn left onto Emley's Hill Road. Parking for Clayton County Park is about 0.3 miles further on the left.

Clayton County Park
Emley's Hill Road
Upper Freehold
Monmouth County
732-842-4000

Mercer County Park

Mercer County Park is located about 7 miles southeast of Princeton and 5 miles northeast of Trenton. With approximately 2,500 acres, it is the largest parcel of bike-accessible public land in the Trenton-Mercer County area. This well-manicured park boasts a tennis complex, a skating rink, and a marina, as well as picnic areas and lighted softball fields.

Mercer's prominence as a first-class mountain-bike destination has grown in recent years, due primarily to the efforts of SMART (Save Mercer and Ride the Trails). Before this organization got involved, Mercer was a vast complex of unmarked and—for the most part—illegally constructed trails. Mountain biking was at best a tolerated activity. Since 1999, this group has been instrumental in defining, marking, and maintaining trails at Mercer.

Many miles of flat, winding singletrack through wooded terrain await the off-road enthusiast at Mercer. While these trails can safely be labeled intermediate, they are best avoided after heavy rains, when traction is difficult and erosion to trail surface likely. Trails are letter coded alphabetically and run from A-X. Unfortunately, on recent rides it seemed that vandalism of trail markers is an ongoing problem in the park; many of the alphabet-coded trail indicators had been tampered with, resulting in possible confusion.

The route maps for this area show two separate rides, connected by a paved multi-use trail accessible from both the East and West Picnic Area parking lots. Indicated directions are to the West Picnic Area parking. It is approximately 1.75 miles via the paved multi-use trail from the West Picnic Area to the East Picnic Area. The mileage indicated for the Mercer County Park (East) ride (5.1) does not include the 1.75 miles of the paved multi-use trail.

If you prefer to drive to the East Picnic Area, leave the West Picnic Area, turn left onto the park road, and follow it to the stop sign. Turn left on Old Trenton Road. At the first traffic light, turn left. The entrance to the East Picnic Area is on the left about a quarter-mile ahead.

Please respect posted no-trespassing signs in the vicinity of the Mercer Oaks Golf Course. This area is off limits to bikes.

Winter warrior

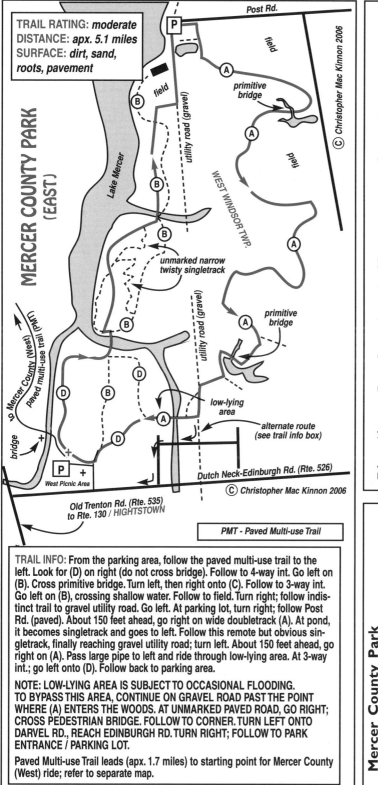

MERCER COUNTY PARK (EAST)

TRAIL RATING: *moderate*
DISTANCE: *apx. 5.1 miles*
SURFACE: *dirt, sand, roots, pavement*

© Christopher Mac Kinnon 2006

Post Rd.

field

Ⓟ

Ⓐ

primitive bridge

Ⓑ field

Ⓐ

field

utility road (gravel)

WEST WINDSOR TWP.

Ⓑ

Lake Mercer

Ⓑ

Ⓐ

unmarked narrow twisty singletrack

Ⓑ

utility road (gravel)

Ⓐ

primitive bridge

Ⓓ

Ⓑ

Ⓐ

low-lying area

Ⓓ

Ⓓ

alternate route (see trail info box)

Mercer County (West) paved multi-use trail (PMT)

bridge

Ⓟ

West Picnic Area

Dutch Neck-Edinburgh Rd. (Rte. 526)

© Christopher Mac Kinnon 2006

Old Trenton Rd. (Rte. 535) to Rte. 130 / HIGHTSTOWN

PMT - Paved Multi-use Trail

TRAIL INFO: From the parking area, follow the paved multi-use trail to the left. Look for (D) on right (do not cross bridge). Follow to 4-way int. Go left on (B). Cross primitive bridge. Turn left, then right onto (C). Follow to 3-way int. Go left on (B), crossing shallow water. Follow to field. Turn right; follow indistinct trail to gravel utility road. Go left. At parking lot, turn right; follow Post Rd. (paved). About 150 feet ahead, go right on wide doubletrack (A). At pond, it becomes singletrack and goes to left. Follow this remote but obvious singletrack, finally reaching gravel utility road; turn left. About 150 feet ahead, go right on (A). Pass large pipe to left and ride through low-lying area. At 3-way int.; go left onto (D). Follow back to parking area.

NOTE: LOW-LYING AREA IS SUBJECT TO OCCASIONAL FLOODING. TO BYPASS THIS AREA, CONTINUE ON GRAVEL ROAD PAST THE POINT WHERE (A) ENTERS THE WOODS. AT UNMARKED PAVED ROAD, GO RIGHT; CROSS PEDESTRIAN BRIDGE. FOLLOW TO CORNER. TURN LEFT ONTO DARVEL RD., REACH EDINBURGH RD. TURN RIGHT; FOLLOW TO PARK ENTRANCE / PARKING LOT.

Paved Multi-use Trail leads (apx. 1.7 miles) to starting point for Mercer County (West) ride; refer to separate map.

Directions: From Route 1 south of Princeton, exit at Quaker Bridge Road (Route 533). Take Quaker Bridge Road south for about 2 miles to Hughes Road. Turn left onto Hughes Road and follow it for about a half mile, turning left onto the main road through Mercer County Park. Follow this road to the West Picnic Area parking lot.

Mercer County Park
Hughes Road
Hamilton, Lawrence, and West Windsor Townships
Mercer County
609-989-6530

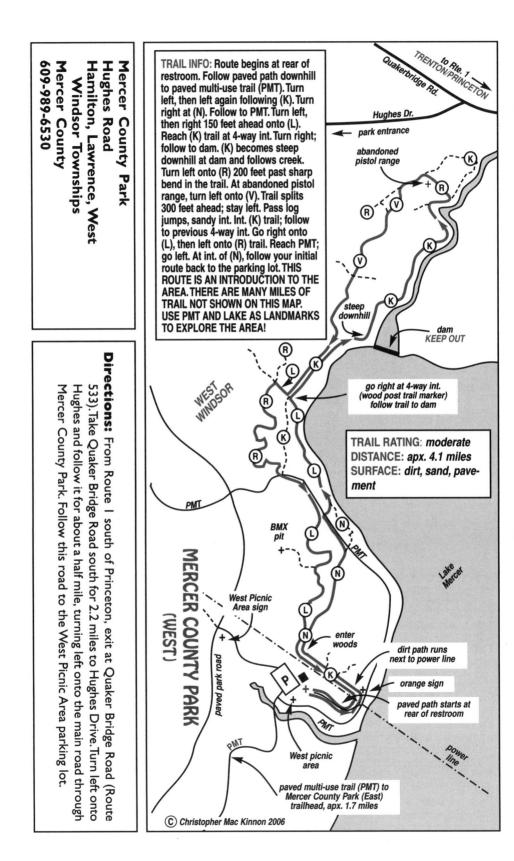

Mercer County Park
Hughes Road
Hamilton, Lawrence, West
Windsor Townships
Mercer County
609-989-6530

TRAIL INFO: Route begins at rear of restroom. Follow paved path downhill to paved multi-use trail (PMT). Turn left, then left again following (K). Turn right at (N). Follow to PMT. Turn left, then right 150 feet ahead onto (L). Reach (K) trail at 4-way int. Turn right; follow to dam. (K) becomes steep downhill at dam and follows creek. Turn left onto (R) 200 feet past sharp bend in the trail. At abandoned pistol range, turn left onto (V). Trail splits 300 feet ahead; stay left. Pass log jumps, sandy int. Int. (K) trail; follow to previous 4-way int. Go right onto (L), then left onto (R) trail. Reach PMT; go left. At int. of (N), follow your initial route back to the parking lot. THIS ROUTE IS AN INTRODUCTION TO THE AREA. THERE ARE MANY MILES OF TRAIL NOT SHOWN ON THIS MAP. USE PMT AND LAKE AS LANDMARKS TO EXPLORE THE AREA!

to Rte. 1
TRENTON/PRINCETON
Quakerbridge Rd.

Hughes Dr.
← park entrance

abandoned pistol range

WEST WINDSOR

steep downhill

dam
KEEP OUT

go right at 4-way int.
(wood post trail marker)
follow trail to dam

TRAIL RATING: *moderate*
DISTANCE: *apx. 4.1 miles*
SURFACE: *dirt, sand, pavement*

PMT

BMX pit

Lake Mercer

MERCER COUNTY PARK
(WEST)

West Picnic Area sign

paved park road

enter woods

dirt path runs next to power line

orange sign

paved path starts at rear of restroom

P

power line

West picnic area

PMT

paved multi-use trail (PMT) to Mercer County Park (East) trailhead, apx. 1.7 miles

© Christopher Mac Kinnon 2006

Directions: From Route 1 south of Princeton, exit at Quaker Bridge Road (Route 533). Take Quaker Bridge Road south for 2.2 miles to Hughes Drive. Turn left onto Hughes and follow it for about a half mile, turning left onto the main road through Mercer County Park. Follow this road to the West Picnic Area parking lot.

Washington Crossing State Park

Washington Crossing State Park, a well-known historical destination, only recently has opened some of its trails to mountain bikes.

The park-designated bike route begins at the Phillips Farm area off Route 579 (Bear Tavern Road). There are several farm buildings adjacent to the parking lot. To find the trail, go behind the buildings and look for a brown trail sign. A green-and-white trail sign should be visible in the distance where the field ends and the woods begin. Follow the grassy path around the perimeter of the field to this point. With the addition of new markers, it has become somewhat easier to navigate through this area.

At the point where the grassy path intersects a gravel road, go around the gate and turn left onto Brickyard Road. (Refer to map inset "B.") Follow Brickyard Road until you reach the main paved road through the park. (Refer to inset "A.") If time permits, stop at the park visitor center, where you'll find exhibits illustrating the historical significance of George Washington's crossing of the Delaware River with the Continental Army on Christmas in 1776, a turning point in the Revolutionary War.

When you're done, take the park road back to Brick Yard Road and follow it to the interpretive center, which houses a collection of exhibits relating to many varieties of wildlife in the park and around New Jersey.

From the interpretive center, backtrack again to Brickyard Road. At this point, the singletrack portion of the ride begins and ends. (Refer to the map for the route through this segment.) When you find yourself back where the singletrack section started, turn left onto Brickyard Road, then left again past the gate, following the gravel road back to the Phillips Farm area.

This ride is rated as moderate because of the singletrack section. Both the road and grassy paths are suited for the casual rider.

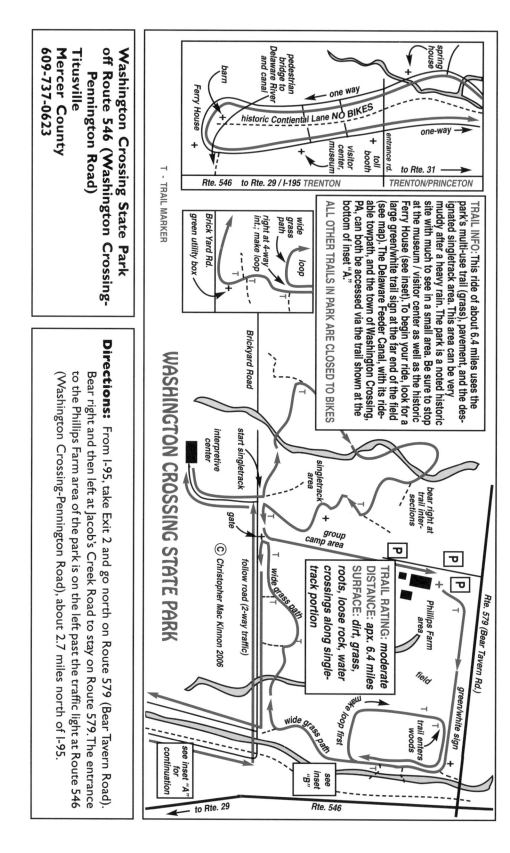

WASHINGTON CROSSING STATE PARK

Washington Crossing State Park
off Route 546 (Washington Crossing-
Pennington Road)
Titusville
Mercer County
609-737-0623

Directions: From I-95, take Exit 2 and go north on Route 579 (Bear Tavern Road). Bear right and then left at Jacob's Creek Road to stay on Route 579. The entrance to the Phillips Farm area of the park is on the left past the traffic light at Route 546 (Washington Crossing-Pennington Road), about 2.7 miles north of I-95.

TRAIL INFO: This ride of about 6.4 miles uses the park's multi-use trail (grass), pavement, and the designated singletrack area. This area can be very muddy after a heavy rain. The park is a noted historic site with much to see in a small area. Be sure to stop at the museum / visitor center as well as the historic Ferry House (see inset). To begin your ride, look for a large green/white trail sign at the far end of the field (see map). The Delaware Feeder Canal, with its rideable towpath, and the town of Washington Crossing, PA, can both be accessed via the trail shown at the bottom of inset "A."
ALL OTHER TRAILS IN PARK ARE CLOSED TO BIKES

TRAIL RATING: *moderate*
DISTANCE: *apx. 6.4 miles*
SURFACE: *dirt, grass, roots, loose rock, water crossings along single-track portion*

T - TRAIL MARKER

© Christopher Mac Kinnon 2006

Rte. 546   to Rte. 29 / I-195 TRENTON   TRENTON/PRINCETON

spring house
pedestrian bridge to Delaware River and canal
barn
one way
Ferry House
historic Contiental Lane NO BIKES
one-way
entrance rd.
toll booth
visitor center, museum
to Rte. 31

wide grass path
right at 4-way int.; make loop
loop
Brick Yard Rd.
green utility box

Brickyard Road
start singletrack
interpretive center
singletrack area
bear right at trail intersections
gate
group camp area
follow road (2-way traffic)
wide grass path

P   P   P
Phillips Farm area
field
greenwhite sign
trail enters woods
make loop first
wide grass path
see inset "A" for continuation
Rte. 579 (Bear Tavern Rd.)
see inset "B"
to Rte. 29
Rte. 546

Sign at Washington Crossing State Park

Smithville star bicycle

Historic Smithville County Park

Historic Smithville County Park packs a diverse collection of recreational opportunities into a relatively small (280-acre) package. Among the facilities available here are hiking and biking trails, picnic areas, fishing sites, and canoe access to Rancocas Creek.

The described route takes you along a cinder and paved trail passing through the Smithville Historic District. Now restored and open to the public, this once-thriving village was a focal point of industry in Burlington County from the 1860s until the 1920s.

Its skilled labor force produced both the high-wheeled bicycle as well as the unique machinery used in operating the Smithville-Mount Holly Bicycle Railroad. An oddity in transportation, this was designed to allow workers to pedal their way from Mount Holly to the H.B. Smith Machine Company in Smithville.

More information about the history of the village is available at the Smith Mansion museum complex, which is located along this route.

A more recent unique feature of this park is the "floating bridge," part of the park's green trail, which crosses 22-acre Smithville Lake. Historic Smithville Park has 4.4 miles of marked trails, most of which are open to bikes, though cyclists are required to dismount at boardwalks and stairs. (The 0.9-mile Ravine Nature Trail is designated for hikers only.)

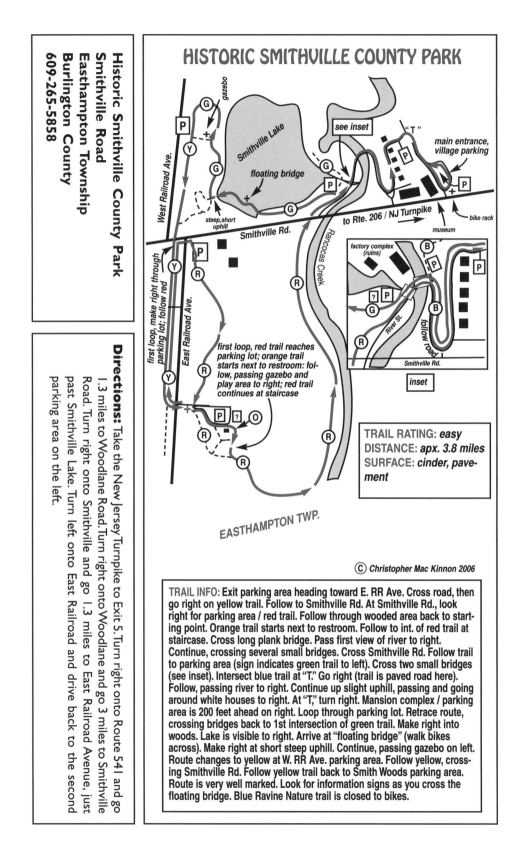

HISTORIC SMITHVILLE COUNTY PARK

Smithville Lake

floating bridge

gazebo

West Railroad Ave.

steep, short uphill

Smithville Rd.

East Railroad Ave.

first loop, make right through parking lot; follow red

first loop, red trail reaches parking lot; orange trail starts next to restroom: follow, passing gazebo and play area to right; red trail continues at staircase

see inset

"T"

main entrance, village parking

to Rte. 206 / NJ Turnpike

bike rack

museum

Rancocas Creek

EASTHAMPTON TWP.

inset

factory complex (ruins)

River St.

follow road

Smithville Rd.

inset

TRAIL RATING: *easy*
DISTANCE: *apx. 3.8 miles*
SURFACE: *cinder, pavement*

© *Christopher Mac Kinnon 2006*

Historic Smithville County Park
Smithville Road
Easthampton Township
Burlington County
609-265-5858

Directions: Take the New Jersey Turnpike to Exit 5. Turn right onto Route 541 and go 1.3 miles to Woodlane Road. Turn right onto Woodlane and go 3 miles to Smithville Road. Turn right onto Smithville and go 1.3 miles to East Railroad Avenue, just past Smithville Lake. Turn left onto East Railroad and drive back to the second parking area on the left.

TRAIL INFO: Exit parking area heading toward E. RR Ave. Cross road, then go right on yellow trail. Follow to Smithville Rd. At Smithville Rd., look right for parking area / red trail. Follow through wooded area back to starting point. Orange trail starts next to restroom. Follow to int. of red trail at staircase. Cross long plank bridge. Pass first view of river to right. Continue, crossing several small bridges. Cross Smithville Rd. Follow trail to parking area (sign indicates green trail to left). Cross two small bridges (see inset). Intersect blue trail at "T." Go right (trail is paved road here). Follow, passing river to right. Continue up slight uphill, passing and going around white houses to right. At "T," turn right. Mansion complex / parking area is 200 feet ahead on right. Loop through parking lot. Retrace route, crossing bridges back to 1st intersection of green trail. Make right into woods. Lake is visible to right. Arrive at "floating bridge" (walk bikes across). Make right at short steep uphill. Continue, passing gazebo on left. Route changes to yellow at W. RR Ave. parking area. Follow yellow, crossing Smithville Rd. Follow yellow trail back to Smith Woods parking area. Route is very well marked. Look for information signs as you cross the floating bridge. Blue Ravine Nature trail is closed to bikes.

Trail marker at Brendan T. Byrne State Forest

Brendan T. Byrne State Forest

The 34,000-acre Brendan T. Byrne State Forest is New Jersey's second-largest state forest, second only to Wharton in size, and it offers virtually unlimited opportunities for off-road exploration. This ride uses only a small portion of the trails and paved and dirt roads within this expansive forest.

This ride follows parts of the paved bike route and cinder paths as well as dirt roads and several unpaved trails as it winds past cranberry bogs, a reservoir, and Lebanon Lake as well as the smaller Pakim Pond, whose name is derived from the Native American word for cranberry. The landscape is quite different here today from the cleared forest that resulted from cutting trees down to provide fuel for a once-thriving glass industry; the glass plant eventually closed when the trees ran out.

In addition to the seemingly endless sea of pines in the forest today, there are clusters of majestic cedar trees which thrive in a wet and sandy environment. Cranberries still thrive and are harvested in some parts of the forest by farmers who lease land from the state.

In a different section of the forest but a short drive away from this ride lies historic Whitesbog Village, a company town that was the birthplace of the commercial blueberry industry. Stop at the park office for directions.

Brendan T. Byrne State Forest was formerly known as Lebanon State Forest, but it was renamed in 2002 to honor the former governor who was responsible for taking steps in the 1970s to protect the Pinelands.

BRENDAN T. BYRNE STATE FOREST

TRAIL INFO: Follow solid red marked cranberry trail to int. of bar red cranberry spur; go right. At 4-way int., go straight, now following solid red markings. Continue, crossing stream, passing white trail. Make left at gate onto Coopers Rd. Pass white trail, continue straight through 3-way int. Cross two streams, go right at paved road (orange bike route). Pass bog, go right on white trail. Follow white markings to Muddy Rd. go left. Follow Muddy Rd. to paved int. (orange bike route). Continue, passing gauging station, then bear left at paved int. Pass white trail and cranberry bog. Make left onto Coopers Rd. Cross two previous small streams, make right onto dirt road; red markings reappear. Follow red markings back to initial 4-way int. Go right; follow marked route back to parking area. NOTE: The multi-use route (white) shown on the park map varies from single to doubletrack, from dirt to sand, and from open to overgrown. The route shown on this map crosses this trail at numerous places along the way.

© Christopher Mac Kinnon 2006

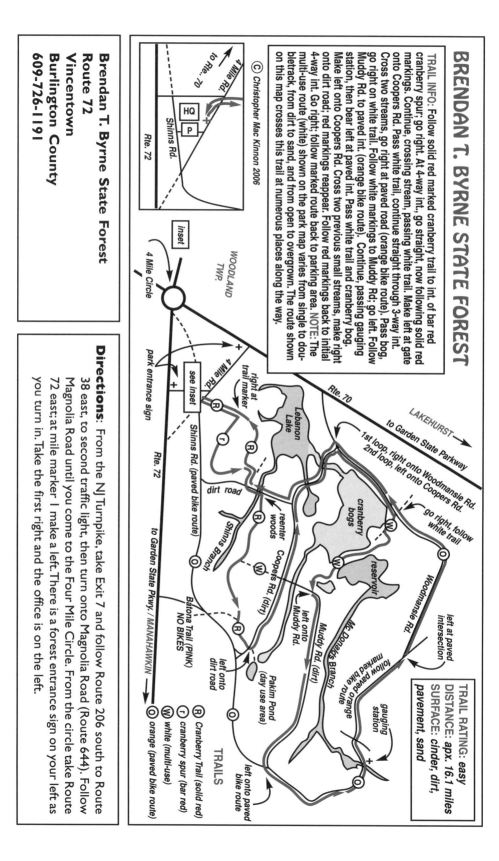

TRAIL RATING: easy
DISTANCE: apx. 16.1 miles
SURFACE: cinder, dirt, pavement, sand

TRAILS

- **R** Cranberry Trail (solid red)
- **r** cranberry spur (bar red)
- **W** white (multi-use)
- **O** orange (paved bike route)

Brendan T. Byrne State Forest
Route 72
Vincentown
Burlington County
609-726-1191

Directions: From the NJ Turnpike, take Exit 7 and follow Route 206 south to Route 38 east, to second traffic light, then turn onto Magnolia Road (Route 644). Follow Magnolia Road until you come to the Four Mile Circle. From the circle take Route 72 east; at mile marker 1 make a left. There is a forest entrance sign on your left as you turn in. Take the first right and the office is on the left.

Cattus Island County Park

Bicycling is just one of many activities available at Cattus Island County Park. This bayside recreation facility also offers birding, crabbing, fishing, slide shows, boat trips, and guided nature walks.

The area has been preserved thanks to the foresight of a number of environmentally concerned individuals including the Cooper family, after whom the Cooper Environmental Center is named. Cattus Island, which is actually a peninsula jutting out into Barnegat Bay, provides a view back in time showing how much of the bay area once looked, and it exists today as both a reminder of the past and a shining example of ecosystem preservation.

The park's 500 acres of salt marshes and wetlands contain 6 miles of well-marked trails, but unfortunately the trail system at Cattus has been designated for foot travel only, so these trails are off limits to bicycling. Cyclists are allowed on the dirt road that runs through the park, which is short but definitely worth including in your visit. The road is closed to vehicular traffic, flat, and relatively smooth, making it ideal for even the most novice rider.

No visit to Cattus would be complete without a walk through the nature center. Here you will find hands-on displays ranging from area topographic maps to antique bay paraphernalia to artwork depicting wildlife native to the park. A well-versed staff of county naturalists and volunteers is available to answer questions.

During the warm-weather months, be sure to bring insect repellant—you'll find a large population of flies and mosquitoes among Cattus Island's many inhabitants!

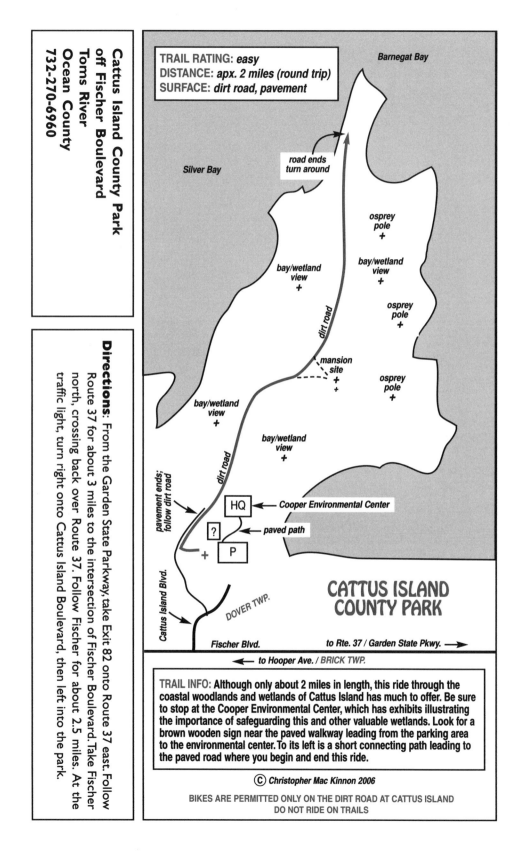

Cattus Island County Park
off Fischer Boulevard
Toms River
Ocean County
732-270-6960

Directions: From the Garden State Parkway, take Exit 82 onto Route 37 east. Follow Route 37 for about 3 miles to the intersection of Fischer Boulevard. Take Fischer north, crossing back over Route 37. Follow Fischer for about 2.5 miles. At the traffic light, turn right onto Cattus Island Boulevard, then left into the park.

TRAIL RATING: *easy*
DISTANCE: *apx. 2 miles (round trip)*
SURFACE: *dirt road, pavement*

Barnegat Bay

Silver Bay

road ends
turn around

osprey
pole
+

bay/wetland
view
+

bay/wetland
view
+

osprey
pole
+

dirt road

mansion
site
+
+

osprey
pole
+

bay/wetland
view
+

bay/wetland
view
+

dirt road

pavement ends;
follow dirt road

HQ ← Cooper Environmental Center

? ← paved path

P

+

Cattus Island Blvd.

DOVER TWP.

**CATTUS ISLAND
COUNTY PARK**

Fischer Blvd.

to Rte. 37 / Garden State Pkwy. ⟶

⟵ to Hooper Ave. / *BRICK TWP.*

TRAIL INFO: **Although only about 2 miles in length, this ride through the coastal woodlands and wetlands of Cattus Island has much to offer. Be sure to stop at the Cooper Environmental Center, which has exhibits illustrating the importance of safeguarding this and other valuable wetlands. Look for a brown wooden sign near the paved walkway leading from the parking area to the environmental center. To its left is a short connecting path leading to the paved road where you begin and end this ride.**

Double Trouble State Park

Located southwest of Toms River on the edge of the New Jersey Pine Barrens, Double Trouble State Park is one of the highlights along the New Jersey Coastal Heritage Trail. Developed primarily for touring by car, the "trail" will link historic, cultural, and natural sites along a 300-mile route from Perth Amboy south to Cape May and from Cape May northwest to the Delaware Memorial Bridge.

Double Trouble got its start as a lumbering center in the 1860s, and at its peak as many as 2,500 people were employed there. Eventually, as the swamps were depleted of timber, they were turned into cranberry bogs. The cranberry industry became a vital part of the South Jersey economy toward the end of the 19th century, and at one time, New Jersey held the distinction of being the nation's leading producer of cranberries. (Today it ranks third behind Massachusetts and Wisconsin.)

The historic village at Double Trouble includes a restored sawmill and cranberry packing and sorting house, with several active cranberry bogs nearby. Other activities available at the park include a self-guided nature walk and canoeing on Cedar Creek. This ride goes through just a small portion of the 5,000-acre park on a wide, hard-packed dirt-and-gravel route that is suitable for all bikes with wide tires.

Trail brochures and information about the New Jersey Coastal Heritage Trail can be obtained by writing the New Jersey Division of Travel and Tourism at PO Box 820, Trenton NJ 08625-0820, or by calling 609-777-0885. The official Web site for the trail is at **http://www.nps.gov/neje/home.htm**.

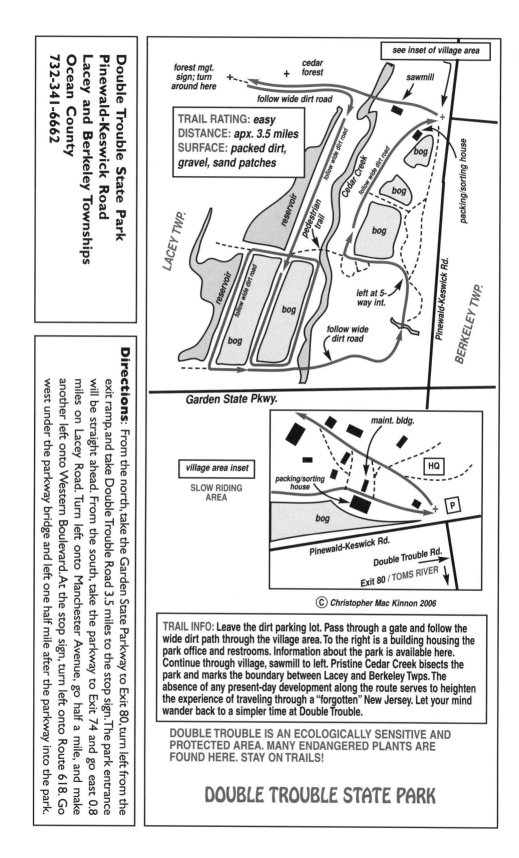

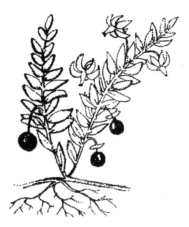

Cranberry plant

The Jersey Devil, a mythical Pinelands creature

Wells Mills County Park

This 900-acre tract in the Pinelands of Ocean County is home to a variety of environments typical of this region. Streams, bogs, swamps, and uplands combine to make the park itself a living museum.

Before beginning your ride, stop by the park office and nature center. The observation deck located in this building provides a panoramic view of the surrounding Pine Barrens. Exhibits in this architecturally appealing structure offer a comprehensive look into Pinelands culture, traditions, and ecosystems.

Wells Mills is the largest park in the Ocean County Park System. It has a total of about 16 miles of trails, but the trails indicated on the route map are the only ones where bikes were permitted at the time of publication. Inquire at the office about whether any additional trails have been designated for or opened to mountain biking.

Ridge and Cooks Mills Roads are easily recognizable, being considerably wider than the numerous intersecting trails. Look for both green blazes and a small metallic sign with a bike symbol and directional arrow.

Wells Mills is a multi-use park. In addition to the network of trails, Wells Mills Lake is open for fishing and boating (electric motors only). The park also rents canoes on a seasonal basis, and the Pine Barrens Jamboree, a celebration of local culture, is held here each October.

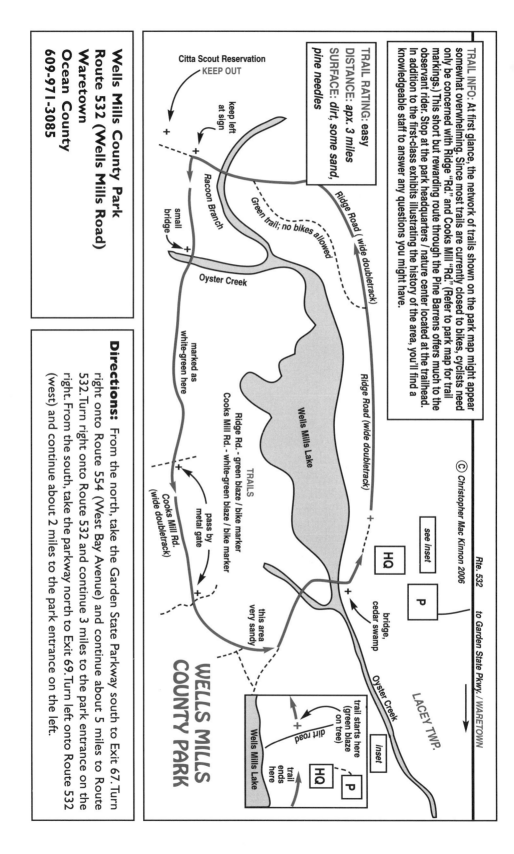

TRAIL INFO: At first glance, the network of trails shown on the park map might appear somewhat overwhelming. Since most trails are currently closed to bikes, cyclists need only be concerned with Ridge "Rd." and Cooks Mill "Rd." (Refer to park map for trail markings.) This short but rewarding route through the Pine Barrens offers much to the observant rider. Stop at the park headquarters / nature center located at the trailhead. In addition to the first-class exhibits illustrating the history of the area, you'll find a knowledgeable staff to answer any questions you might have.

TRAIL RATING: easy
DISTANCE: apx. 3 miles
SURFACE: dirt, some sand, pine needles

Citta Scout Reservation
KEEP OUT

keep left at sign

Racoon Branch

small bridge

Green trail; no bikes allowed

Ridge Road (wide doubletrack)

Oyster Creek

Ridge Road (wide doubletrack)

Wells Mills Lake

marked as white-green here

TRAILS
Ridge Rd. - green blaze / bike marker
Cooks Mill Rd. - white-green blaze / bike marker

pass by metal gate

Cooks Mill Rd. (wide doubletrack)

this area very sandy

© Christopher Mac Kinnon 2006

Rte. 532   to Garden State Pkwy. / WARETOWN

see inset

HQ   P

bridge, cedar swamp

Oyster Creek   LACEY TWP.

inset

trail starts here (green blaze on tree)
dirt road

trail ends here

Wells Mills Lake   HQ   P

WELLS MILLS COUNTY PARK

Wells Mills County Park
Route 532 (Wells Mills Road)
Waretown
Ocean County
609-971-3085

Directions: From the north, take the Garden State Parkway south to Exit 67. Turn right onto Route 554 (West Bay Avenue) and continue about 5 miles to Route 532. Turn right onto Route 532 and continue 3 miles to the park entrance on the right. From the south, take the parkway north to Exit 69. Turn left onto Route 532 (west) and continue about 2 miles to the park entrance on the left.

Parvin State Park

Parvin State Park in Salem County is a prime multi-use recreation area for residents of South Jersey, and it is one of the few sizable tracts of public land in this part of the state where mountain biking is both appealing and allowed.

Along with swimming, hiking, boating, and horseback riding, bicycling is encouraged by the park. Most trails in the park are well suited for riding. The terrain is generally flat and satisfactory for riders at all levels of ability. Trails vary from wide doubletrack to occasional singletrack, along with several paved sections.

I recommend avoiding the section of the Long Trail (red) between its intersections with the Green Trail and a short connector trail. The designated nature trail is located here and it is intended primarily for foot travel. Also, this is a low-lying area that is subject to flooding in wet weather and tends to become overgrown in the warmer months. This area can be bypassed by means of the paved park loop road shown on the map.

Be sure to pick up a park brochure before you start to ride. It shows the complete network of marked trails and facilities and also provides a wealth of information pertaining to the history of the park. Unfortunately, trail markings at Parvin are currently "iffy" at best. A recent ride indicated a lack of trail signage, perhaps the result of vandalism or neglect.

Several of the trails shown on the route map, as well as numerous intersecting trails, are open to both horses and hikers. Please extend courtesy to both to avoid any unnecessary conflicts. Dismounting in the presence of horses is strongly recommended.

During the summer months, the cool waters of Parvin Lake are available for a refreshing swim. Inquire at the office about access to the beach area.

TRAIL INFO: Facing the park office, turn right onto the green trail. At first, the route parallels the fenced day-use area. Follow until you reach paved path. Go left; cross Muddy Creek. Arrive at paved forest loop road; go right. Follow to connector trail (look for bench / small sand pile), 100 feet ahead, int. red trail; go left. Follow through 4-way int. Follow, passing several marked trails; stay on red. At 5-way int., continue straight. Cross bridge and follow yellow trail around lake. At wood platform, leave trail and continue on paved road. Pass cabins. As you make loop, look for Black Oak (brown) Trail sign. Follow double / singletrack trail back to 4-way int. Go through 4-way; arrive at park loop road. Make right and follow back to paved path. Go right on paved path, then right again on green, back to the parking lot.

TRAILS

- Ⓖ *Parvin Lake (green)*
- Ⓡ *Long (red)*
- Ⓨ *Thundergust (yellow)*
- Ⓑ *Black Oak (brown)*
- Ⓑ *Forest Loop (blue)*

Parvin State Park
701 Almond Road
Pittsgrove
Salem County
856-358-8616

Directions: From Route 55, take Exit 35 onto Route 674. Follow Route 674 west 2.1 miles to Route 645. Turn left onto Route 645 and follow it 2 miles to Route 540. Turn right onto Route 540. Use the parking lot on the right, across from the park headquarters and Parvin Lake.

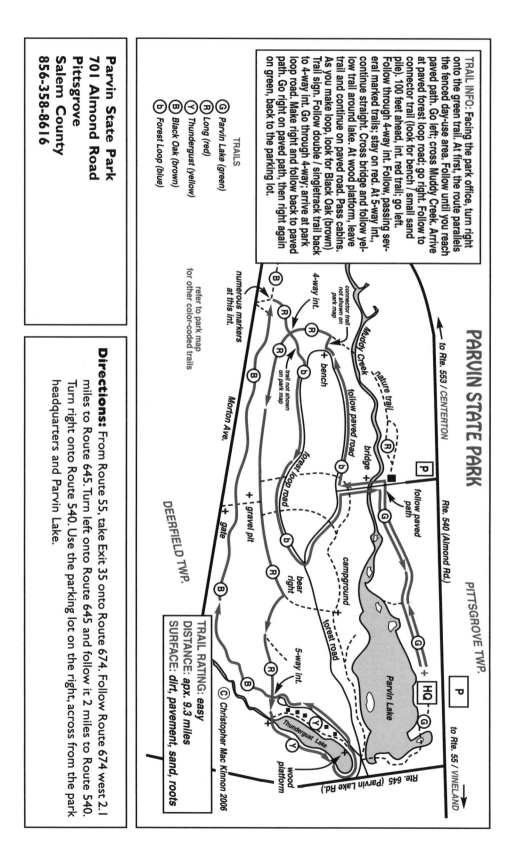

PARVIN STATE PARK

PITTSGROVE TWP.

to Rte. 553 / CENTERTON

to Rte. 55 / VINELAND

Rte. 540 (Almond Rd.)

Muddy Creek

nature trail

bridge

follow paved road

follow paved path

connector trail not shown on park map

4-way int.

numerous markers at this int.

trail not shown on park map

bench

refer to park map for other color-coded trails

Morton Ave.

forest loop road

DEERFIELD TWP.

gravel pit

gate

bear right

campground

forest road

5-way int.

Parvin Lake

Thundergust Lake

wood platform

Rte. 645 (Parvin Lake Rd.)

© Christopher Mac Kinnon 2006

P

HQ

Ⓖ

TRAIL RATING: *easy*
DISTANCE: *apx. 9.3 miles*
SURFACE: *dirt, pavement, sand, roots*

Estell Manor County Park

Atlantic County usually brings to mind images of its most famous destination, Atlantic City, the gambling capital of the East. A visit there is likely to be a win-lose proposition at best.

Nearby Estell Manor County Park, on the other hand, is a sure winner. The nature center and historic points of interest have been drawing visitors for years. Hiking and boating are also popular activities. Now mountain biking can be added to this list.

The Duck Farm Trail, located in the north end of the park, is the end result of thoughtful planning and hard work by members of the Atlantic County Trail Volunteers organization (ACTV; see page 142 for more information about this organization). In 2002, ACTV received final approval to build a singletrack mountain bike route. Thanks to this new trail, a loop route totaling approximately 6 miles, Estell Manor is shaping up as the prime mountain-biking destination in South Jersey.

The trail is located along the coastal lowlands and elevation change is negligible but at the same time incidental, due to the creative layout of the route. A serpentine hard-packed path through a forest of pine, oak, and holly awaits riders of all abilities.

This is a trail built by dedicated mountain bikers for mountain bikers. Horses are prohibited on this trail and should be reported to the park office.

The park office located with the nature center about a mile south on Route 50 can provide updated route maps as well as information regarding the park.

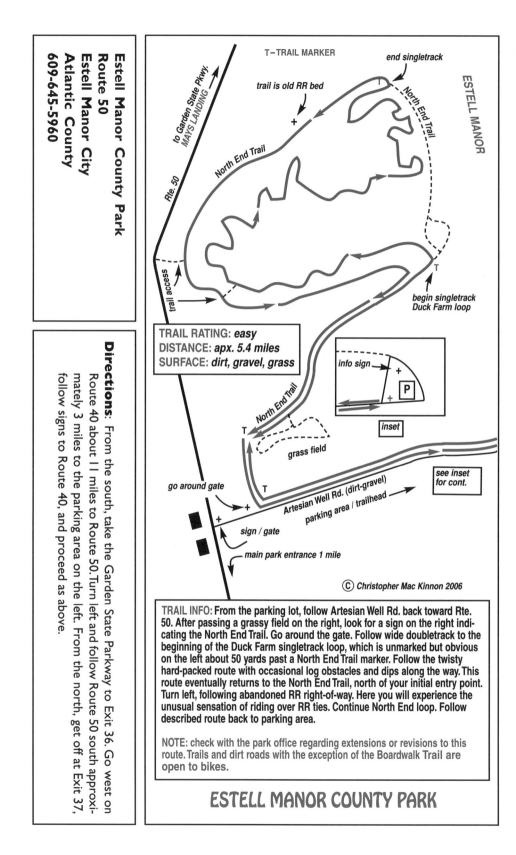

Estell Manor County Park
Route 50
Estell Manor City
Atlantic County
609-645-5960

T–TRAIL MARKER

end singletrack

trail is old RR bed

ESTELL MANOR

North End Trail

to Garden State Pkwy.
MAYS LANDING

Rte. 50

North End Trail

trail access

begin singletrack
Duck Farm loop

T

TRAIL RATING: *easy*
DISTANCE: *apx. 5.4 miles*
SURFACE: *dirt, gravel, grass*

North End Trail

T

T

grass field

info sign

P

inset

go around gate

Artesian Well Rd. (dirt-gravel)
parking area / trailhead

T

see inset
for cont.

sign / gate

main park entrance 1 mile

© *Christopher Mac Kinnon 2006*

Directions: From the south, take the Garden State Parkway to Exit 36. Go west on Route 40 about 11 miles to Route 50. Turn left and follow Route 50 south approximately 3 miles to the parking area on the left. From the north, get off at Exit 37, follow signs to Route 40, and proceed as above.

TRAIL INFO: From the parking lot, follow Artesian Well Rd. back toward Rte. 50. After passing a grassy field on the right, look for a sign on the right indicating the North End Trail. Go around the gate. Follow wide doubletrack to the beginning of the Duck Farm singletrack loop, which is unmarked but obvious on the left about 50 yards past a North End Trail marker. Follow the twisty hard-packed route with occasional log obstacles and dips along the way. This route eventually returns to the North End Trail, north of your initial entry point. Turn left, following abandoned RR right-of-way. Here you will experience the unusual sensation of riding over RR ties. Continue North End loop. Follow described route back to parking area.

NOTE: check with the park office regarding extensions or revisions to this route. Trails and dirt roads with the exception of the Boardwalk Trail are open to bikes.

ESTELL MANOR COUNTY PARK

Atlantic County Bikeway

The Atlantic County Bikeway, which opened in 2002, is one of the latest additions to the growing number of converted railroad rights-of-way in New Jersey. Formerly part of the Pennsylvania-Reading Seashore rail line, it provides a rare opportunity for off-road riding in an area of the state that is rapidly being developed.

The ride begins and ends at the Shore Mall in Egg Harbor Township. The 7.5-mile route passes mostly through residential areas, although there is a stretch that takes you through an undeveloped area devoid of roads and traffic. Oak and pine trees on either side of the trail provide some degree of relief from nearby traffic and housing.

At approximately 0.7 miles, look to the left for a small rectangular sign with a large W. Aside from this single railroad marker, there is little to suggest the path's prior use. Scattered cinders and the occasional decaying railroad tie are other faint reminders from days gone by.

At the intersection of the bikeway and English Creek Road, there is a pedestrian-activated traffic signal to facilitate crossing this busy intersection. All other road crossings use stop signs. Trail mileage is indicated by means of posted markers or numbers painted on the trail surface.

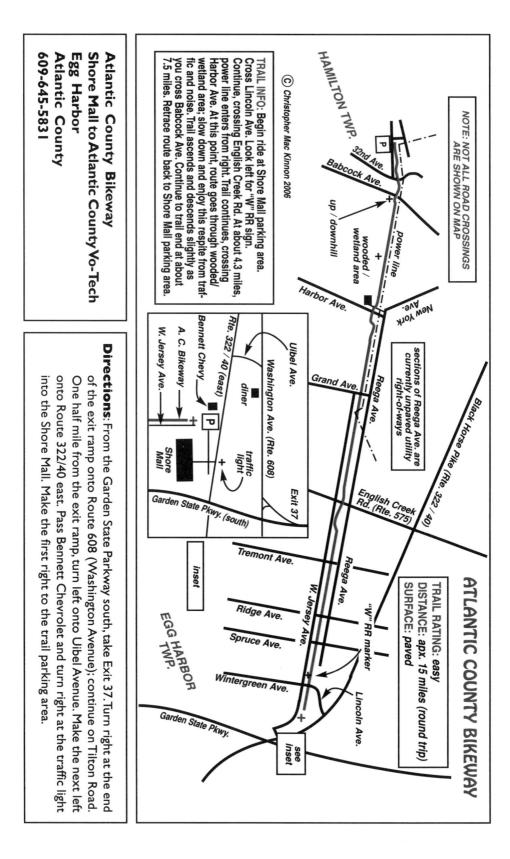

ATLANTIC COUNTY BIKEWAY

TRAIL RATING: *easy*
DISTANCE: *apx. 15 miles (round trip)*
SURFACE: *paved*

NOTE: NOT ALL ROAD CROSSINGS ARE SHOWN ON MAP

© Christopher Mac Kinnon 2006

HAMILTON TWP.

32nd Ave.

Babcock Ave.

up / downhill

power line

wooded / wetland area

P

Harbor Ave.

New York Ave.

sections of Reega Ave. are currently unpaved utility right-of-ways

Grand Ave.

Reega Ave.

Black Horse Pike (Rte. 322 / 40)

English Creek Rd. (Rte. 575)

Tremont Ave.

Reega Ave.

W. Jersey Ave.

"W" RR marker

Ridge Ave.

Spruce Ave.

Wintergreen Ave.

Lincoln Ave.

Garden State Pkwy.

EGG HARBOR TWP.

see inset

TRAIL INFO: Begin ride at Shore Mall parking area. Cross Lincoln Ave. Look left for "W" RR sign. Continue, crossing English Creek Rd. At about 4.3 miles, power line enters from right. Trail continues, crossing Harbor Ave. At this point, route goes through wooded/ wetland area. slow down and enjoy this respite from traffic and noise. Trail ascends and descends slightly as you cross Babcock Ave. Continue to trail end at about 7.5 miles. Retrace route back to Shore Mall parking area.

inset

Rte. 322 / 40 (east)

Bennett Chevy

A. C. Bikeway

W. Jersey Ave.

Uibel Ave.

Washington Ave. (Rte. 608)

diner

traffic light

Shore Mall

Exit 37

Garden State Pkwy. (south)

P

Directions: From the Garden State Parkway south, take Exit 37. Turn right at the end of the exit ramp onto Route 608 (Washington Avenue); continue on Tilton Road. One half mile from the exit ramp, turn left onto Uibel Avenue. Make the next left onto Route 322/40 east. Pass Bennett Chevrolet and turn right at the traffic light into the Shore Mall. Make the first right to the trail parking area.

Atlantic County Bikeway
Shore Mall to Atlantic County Vo-Tech
Egg Harbor
Atlantic County
609-645-5831

Belleplain State Forest

Located at the southern end of the New Jersey Pinelands, Belleplain State Forest is a popular destination for campers. Its recreational opportunities include boating, fishing, picnicking, and swimming from the white sand beaches of beautiful Lake Nummy, a former cranberry bog that was transformed by Civilian Conservation Corps workers during the 1930s. The park has a bathhouse with showers and a food concession.

In addition, there are 40 miles of trails used for hiking, biking, horseback riding, and cross-country skiing in season. Each trail is marked with signs indicating its designated use.

This 15.1-mile route includes paved and unpaved roads and parts of several trails including the East Creek Trail, which connects Lake Nummy with East Creek Pond. It covers varied terrain and is suitable for riders of moderate ability.

Belleplain Forest includes stands of pine, oak, and Atlantic white cedar. It is home to white-tailed deer, red foxes, and ruffed grouse. Unfortunately, the insect population is also thriving here, and cyclists should follow the usual precautions. (See page 18 for more about ticks and Lyme Disease.)

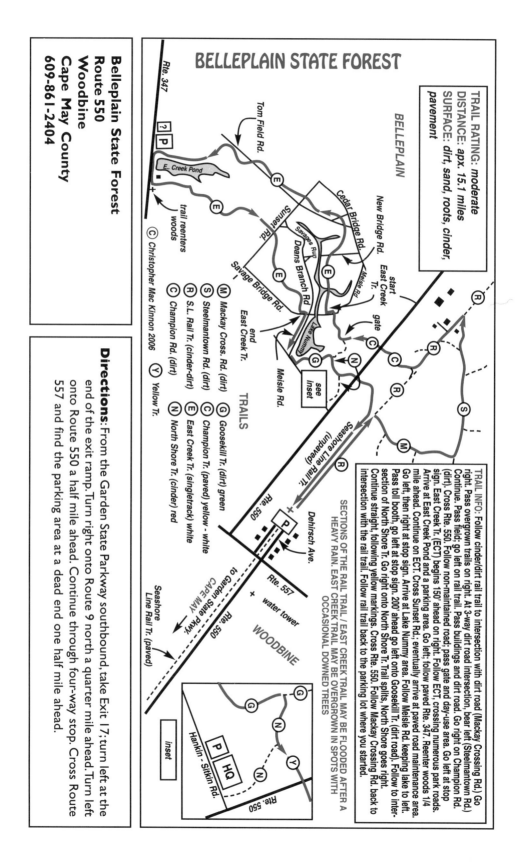

BELLEPLAIN STATE FOREST

TRAIL RATING: *moderate*
DISTANCE: *apx. 15.1 miles*
SURFACE: *dirt, sand, roots, cinder, pavement*

BELLEPLAIN

Rte. 347

Tom Field Rd.

E. Creek Pond

New Bridge Rd.

Cedar Bridge Rd.

Sunset Rd.

Savages Run

Deans Branch Rd.

Meisle Rd.

Savage Bridge Rd.

trail reenters woods

start
East Creek Tr.

gate

end
East Creek Tr.

Meisle Rd.

Lake Nummy

see inset

© Christopher Mac Kinnon 2006

TRAILS

- **(M)** Mackay Cross. Rd. (dirt)
- **(S)** Steelmantown Rd. (dirt)
- **(R)** S.L. Rail Tr. (cinder-dirt)
- **(C)** Champion Rd. (dirt)
- **(G)** Goosekill Tr. (dirt) green
- **(C)** Champion Tr. (paved) yellow - white
- **(E)** East Creek Tr. (singletrack) white
- **(N)** North Shore Tr. (cinder) red
- **(Y)** Yellow Tr.

TRAIL INFO: Follow cinder/dirt rail trail to intersection with dirt road (Mackay Crossing Rd.) Go right. Pass overgrown trails on right. At 3-way dirt road intersection, bear left (Steelmantown Rd.) Continue. Pass field; go left on rail trail. Pass buildings and dirt road. Go right on Champion Rd. (dirt). Cross Rte. 550. Follow non-maintained road; pass gate and day-use area. Go left at stop sign. East Creek Tr. (ECT) begins 150' ahead on right. Follow ECT, crossing numerous park roads. Arrive at East Creek Pond and a parking area. Go left; follow paved Rte. 347. Reenter woods 1/4 mile ahead. Continue on ECT. Cross Sunset Rd.; eventually arrive at paved road maintenance area. Go left, then right at stop sign. Arrive at Lake Nummy area. Follow Meisle Rd. keeping lake to left. Pass toll booth, go left at stop sign. 200 ahead go left onto Goosekill Tr. (dirt road). Follow to intersection of North Shore Tr. Go right onto North Shore Tr. Trail splits, North Shore goes right. Continue straight, following yellow markings. Cross Rte. 550. Follow Mackay Crossing Rd. back to intersection with the rail trail. Follow rail trail back to the parking lot where you started.

SECTIONS OF THE RAIL TRAIL / EAST CREEK TRAIL MAY BE FLOODED AFTER A HEAVY RAIN. EAST CREEK TRAIL MAY BE OVERGROWN IN SPOTS WITH OCCASIONAL DOWNED TREES

Seashore Line Rail Tr. (unpaved)

Rte. 550

Dehirsch Ave.

to Garden State Pkwy.

Rte. 557

water tower

WOODBINE

Rte. 550

Seashore Line Rail Tr. (paved)

CAPE MAY

inset

Hankin - Sitkin Rd.

P   HQ

Rte. 550

Belleplain State Forest
Route 550
Woodbine
Cape May County
609-861-2404

Directions: From the Garden State Parkway southbound, take Exit 17; turn left at the end of the exit ramp. Turn right onto Route 9 north a quarter mile ahead. Turn left onto Route 550 a half mile ahead. Continue through four-way stop. Cross Route 557 and find the parking area at a dead end one half mile ahead.

Trail marker at Belleplain State Forest

Get involved

By designing and maintaining trails and educating trail users, bike advocacy groups have played a major role in the success our sport enjoys today. These organizations depend on the contributions of many dedicated volunteers to accomplish their goals.

Two national cycling-advocacy organizations have led the way:

International Mountain Bicycling Association (IMBA)
www.imba.com

National Off-Road Bicycling Association (NORBA)
www.usacycling.org/mtb/

This group is active on the state level:

Jersey Off-Road Bicycling Association (JORBA)
www.jorba.info

A number of regional or local groups share the objectives of these larger organizations:

Allaire Trail Users Group (ATUG)
http://www.bicyclehub.com/NJCCC/atug.htm

A coalition of bikers, hikers, hunters, and equestrians who have come together to work for a common cause. ATUG is responsible for maintaining existing trails at the park and has been instrumental in the design and construction of new trails.

Save Mercer and Ride the Trails (SMART)
www.angelfire.com/nj2/smart17/

A mountain-bike advocacy group dedicated to maintaining and improving the off-road trails in Mercer County Park in West Windsor. The organization schedules regular trail-maintenance days on the third Saturday of each month.

Atlantic County Trail Volunteers (ACTV)
www.geocities.com/actv03/

A volunteer organization that has brought together recreational mountain bikers and hikers to address trail issues in Atlantic County. The organization designs, builds, and maintains environmentally conscious and safe singletrack trail systems.

Contact us

Let us know what you think of these routes. Tell us if trail conditions have changed, or if you have new information to add. We'll post any updates we receive on the Freewheeling Press website.

Also, tell us about your own favorite bicycling routes. (They don't have to be in New Jersey.) Rides suggested by readers may be included on our website or in future editions of this or other bicycle tour books.

Write to us at:

Freewheeling Press
P.O. Box 540
Lahaska PA 18931

You can also reach us via e-mail:

info@freewheelingpress.com

You'll find useful information about bicycling in New Jersey and news about what's happening here at Freewheeling Press on our website:

www.freewheelingpress.com

Buy a book

Use this form to order books from Freewheeling Press, or look for more information about ordering online at www.freewheelingpress.com.

Name:			
Address:			
Telephone:			

No.	Title	Price	Total
	Back Roads Bicycling in Bucks County, Pa. *Features more than 40 rides on bike paths and scenic roads, with detailed maps and descriptions in a bike-friendly format.*	$14.95	
	Mountain Biking in New Jersey *Third edition with 50 off-road rides in the Garden State, each accompanied by descriptive text and a detailed map showing everything you need to know to enjoy the ride.*	$16.95	
	Walking Bucks County, Pa. *A guide to walks on country roads, paved paths, and woodland trails in this scenic area, with maps.*	$12.95	
	Freewheeling Press Bike Journal *Personal bike touring journal opens flat for easy writing, with space to record directions, distance, difficulty, and other details of your rides.*	$12.95	
	The Back Roads Bike Book *Maps and directions for a dozen short scenic rides in and around Lambertville, N.J., and New Hope, Pa., with info on things to see and do, places to stay.*	$12.95	

Send to: **Freewheeling Press** **PO Box 540** **Lahaska PA 18931**		
	Shipping ($3 per book)	
	Subtotal	
	Pa. residents add 6% tax	
	Grand total	
	Make check payable to Freewheeling Press	